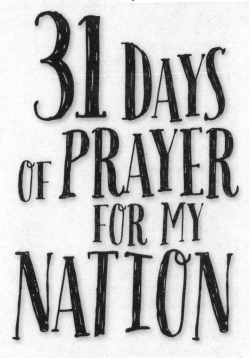

31 DAYS OF PRAYER FOR MY NATION

ABRIDGED

BroadStreet
PUBLISHING

Contents

Foreword

I believe it is imperative for every Christian and church to pray for our nation. I believe this is biblical, therefore, must be convictional.

America has never needed Christians and churches to pray for our nation more. This is why we are putting this book, *31 Days of Prayer for My Nation,* into your hands.

Please join me, along with thousands of Christians and churches in America, as we allocate thirty-one days to pray in agreement for our nation. As we prepare to enter this journey, let's make every effort to gather other Christians and churches to join us.

Now is the time to pray for America. Now is the time for every spiritual leader to consider standing with me and others, calling upon people from all walks of life to pray for our nation. Whether you are a pastor of a local church, a leader in a denomination, or a leader in your fellowship of believers, let's do all we can to come together and pray for our nation.

Distance may separate us physically, but our oneness in Christ will unite us spiritually. As we enter prayerful intercession for our nation, may this be the time when God answers our prayers and the next great spiritual awakening occurs.

Let's agree clearly, unite visibly, and pray extraordinarily for the revival of the church and the awakening of the nation spiritually, so we can see the gospel of Jesus Christ advanced to every person globally.

Dr. Ronnie Floyd
President, National Day of Prayer

 Scan here to learn more about the purpose of this book and its collection of resources.

DAY 1

Why Pray for My Nation?

Make every effort to keep yourselves united in the Spirit,
binding yourselves together with peace.

EPHESIANS 4:3

U nity is our only hope for all that divides us. Jesus prayed, "I pray that they will all be one, just as you and I are one—as you are in me, Father, and I am in you. And may they be in us so that the world will believe you sent me" (John 17:21).

☆ Lord, regardless of our own preferences or traditions, draw each of your followers together as a witness of Jesus to the entire world.

☆ Father, use your church to serve as the unifying body of people in our nation.

☆ Holy Spirit, wake up your church to spiritual revival, experiencing the manifest presence of God as a people.

Our leaders must turn toward His Word and will: "The king's heart is like a stream of water directed by the LORD; he guides it wherever he pleases" (Proverbs 21:1).

☆ Lord Jesus, we ask you to turn the heart of our president, vice president, and both houses of Congress toward your Word and your ways.

☆ Father, we ask you to inspire and lead the hearts of our political leaders to come together for the good of our nation.

☆ Holy Spirit, we ask you to place God's armor upon each of our leaders, protecting them and their families in every way.

The truth is that the next great spiritual awakening can usher in the fulfillment of the Great Commission. This is why Paul reminds us, "This is all the more urgent, for you know how late it is; time is running out. Wake up, for our salvation is nearer now than when we first believed" (Romans 13:11).

☆ Father, we ask that your sovereign will be for the next great spiritual awakening to occur in our generation.

☆ Lord Jesus, because of your grace, pour out your power upon our nation, bringing forth a spiritual awakening that will result in millions coming to faith in Jesus Christ.

☆ Holy Spirit, move your church to pray extraordinarily until we see the next great spiritual awakening in our generation.

DAY 2

What to Pray for My Nation

Our God can do anything, anytime, anywhere, with anyone. God can do more in a moment than you could ever do in a lifetime.

THREE PRAYER PRIORITIES FOR UNITY

Whether you pray daily or weekly for our nation, please join in praying with the authority of the Scriptures for these three priorities for our nation:

PRAY FOR UNITY IN OUR NATION (#PRAY4UNITY)

Make every effort to keep the unity of the Spirit through the bond of peace. (Ephesians 4:3 NIV)

☆ Father in heaven, you are the only one who can bring unity, harmony, and oneness in our nation. We pray and ask you for unity in our nation.

☆ Lord, call the churches of our nation to live in unity within their own church and in unity with churches that are biblically based and Jesus-centered.

☆ Jesus, as your church walks in unity, harmony, and oneness, may your church personify, lead, and call our nation to unity.

☆ Lord Jesus Christ, in this crisis moment in our nation, it is incumbent upon each of us to come together for the sake of the gospel, the testimony of the gospel, and the global advancement of the gospel; consequently, God, may we *make every* effort to unite in prayer and pursuit of your purpose for this nation.

☆ Father, while our nation is filled with so many challenges and divisions abound, use each of us to unify our families, our churches, our workplaces, and our communities.

TRUST GOD TO LEAD OUR NATION THROUGH THESE CRITICAL TIMES OF DECISION-MAKING

"For I know the plans I have for you," says the LORD. "They are plans for good and not for disaster, to give you a future and a hope." (Jeremiah 29:11)

☆ Lord, we trust you to convict our nation's leaders of your desire for them to work together in unity for the well-being of our nation.

☆ Sovereign Lord, we appeal to you alone to give our nation a future and a hope.

☆ Spirit of God, move upon the leaders of our nation to work together toward resolving the following issues for the welfare of our nation: tax reform, health-care reform, immigration reform, national security, religious liberty, sanctity and dignity of human life, and terrorism (both nationally and globally).

☆ Lord and Defender, we appeal to you to protect the leaders of our nation and their families, as well as the members of our military, both nationally and globally, and all the first responders in our nation.

BELIEVE GOD FOR HIS SUPERNATURAL INTERVENTION IN OUR NATION ON THE NATIONAL DAY OF PRAYER (THE FIRST THURSDAY OF EACH MAY)

In those days when you pray, I will listen. If you look for me wholeheartedly, you will find me. (Jeremiah 29:12–13)

☆ Lord, on this day when millions of people gather in thousands of settings, please listen to our prayers as we seek you with all our hearts.

☆ Father, in these most critical moments in our generation, please call leaders of denominations, churches, government, education, business, cities, and all communities in our nation to create numerous gatherings that will saturate their regions in prayer for unity in our nation.

DAY 3

How to Pray for My Nation

*"I looked for someone who might rebuild the wall…
to stand in the gap…so I wouldn't have to destroy the land,
but I found no one."*

EZEKIEL 22:30

It is the people in God's house who hold the future of our nation, not governmental leaders. We are called to pray for those in authority but not to depend upon them for the healing of our nation.

God has been filled with grace and mercy toward a nation characterized by a lack of biblical truth. Believers *know* the truth, but it does no good if that truth doesn't live fully within them and if it is not expressed in their everyday lives. Crisis in our nation will not be averted through an election but only because the people, who are called by His name, have humbled themselves and prayed, sought His face, and turned from their wicked ways (see 2 Chronicles 7:14).

If our dependence is on God, then we will continue to seek Him on behalf of our nation despite any election results. The church has been impotent and silent before heaven, as well as within our culture. We have been relegated to the position of irrelevance, and so has our God. His people have not represented Him in the fight for biblical truth in our nation, and we are now reaping what we have sown.

But God …

If we, who are His people and who are called by His name, will truly humble ourselves and pray, seek His face, and turn from our wicked ways, then He will hear from heaven, forgive our sins, and heal our land. What an incredible promise that has been left unclaimed in this generation.

It's time to blow the trumpet and sound the alarm (see Joel 2). Believers must not stop seeking the face of God until revival is poured out upon a repentant people and His kingdom is unmistakably established within our nation once again.

The future of our nation is teetering on a precipice, and our response to this perilous moment in history will reveal the true condition of our hearts. May our God find us faithfully about the work of earnest and focused intercession so that He will hear the prayers from His humble, broken people, pour out His merciful forgiveness, and heal our land.

DAY 4

Our Nation Is Broken

"…an humble attempt to promote explicit agreement and visible union of God's people in extraordinary prayer for the revival of religion and the advancement of Christ's Kingdom on earth…."

JONATHAN EDWARDS

Prayer is imperative because our nation is broken. Division is undeniable and unity is missing. Racial tension is alarming. Lawlessness abounds. Reconciliation appears impossible.

Government cannot fix us. Politics will not heal us. We need God now more than at any time in our generation.

It is prayer that precedes and forwards the advancement of the gospel. It is prayer that precedes any great movement of God. In fact, it is prayer that will precede the revival of the church and the next great spiritual awakening.

In this desperate and urgent hour, when turmoil and division are evident in our nation and security threats are very real, it is imperative that we do all we can to mobilize unified public prayer for our nation.

Paul writes, "Make every effort to keep the unity of the Spirit through the bond of peace" (Ephesians 4:3 NIV). The present spiritual crisis is calling us to pray for and take all the necessary actions to come together as a nation. God is the only one who can bring unity, harmony, and oneness to our country; therefore, we look only to Him in prayer.

Call upon God to empower us to make every effort to live in unity, call for unity, and to promote unity in our nation continually.

THANKS

☆ *Give thanks to the Father:* Father, we have been abundantly blessed by your hand upon our nation; I rejoice and give thanks for the divine favor and protection that you have provided.

CONFESSION

☆ *Listen for the Holy Spirit's prompting for confession:* Forgive us that we have too often received your grace and favor in vain; we repent of looking for manmade solutions to struggles that need your divine touch. Turn our eyes and hearts back to you, beginning with me.

PETITION

☆ *Join Jesus in prayers of petition:* Continue to pour out your grace; hold back your judgment as you unite your people in prevailing prayer for revival in your church and spiritual awakening in the nation.

WORD

☆ ***Proclaim promises from His Word:*** Open eyes to see
and hearts to embrace that "God's kindness is intended
to lead you to repentance" (Romans 2:4 NIV).

ENGAGE

☆ **Engage with other Jesus-followers in a lifestyle of
prayer:** Become actively involved in the ministries of
the National Day of Prayer, encouraging your pastor
and church to become fully engaged.

> SPIRIT-
> EMPOWERED
> *Faith*
>
> **Love the Lord L-1:**
> Spirit-empowered disciples love the Lord through
> practicing thanksgiving in all things.

DAY 5

Why Unity Matters
The Heart of Jesus

*We are on the precipice of either experiencing awakening
or falling into an abyss.*

In one of the few recorded prayers we have of Jesus, He prayed
specifically for unity of His future followers: "I pray that
they will all be one ..." (John 17:21). Why did He want that? He
went on to pray, "May they experience such perfect unity that
the world will know that you sent me and that you love them as
much as you love me" (John 17:23).

First Timothy 2:1–4 indicates that God's desire is for
all people to be saved. And that happens best—accord-
ing to Scripture—when His people are in unity, working,

fellowshipping, and praying together.

Looking historically at revival and spiritual awakening in the United States, we find that a key element that launched those moves of God was unity. Churches started praying together, seeking God for their communities and nation. In the prayer meeting revival of the late 1850s, believers from many different churches started meeting in noontime prayer meetings across cities, not caring about the "tribes" with which they shouldn't mingle. That had a common goal and vision.

God is at work to tear down those walls that divide the denominational (and nondenominational) tribes for the sake of the gospel. Pastors need to be less concerned about what intermingling might do to theological purity and be more concerned with what unity will do for the sake of lost souls.

THANKS

☆ **Give thanks to the Father:** I praise and thank you, Lord Jesus, that in you "we are many parts of one body, and we all belong to each other" (Romans 12:5)

CONFESSION

☆ **Listen for the Holy Spirit's prompting for confession:** Forgive me, Lord, for not crossing barriers to love beyond my comfort zone; extend your life and love through me to those unlike me.

PETITION

☆ **Join Jesus in prayers of petition:** Father God, help us to keep our focus on eternal priorities, that in them we might "all agree and that there be no divisions among [us]" (1 Corinthians 1:10 NASB).

WORD

☆ **Proclaim promises from His Word:** Holy Spirit, make my life an answer to the high-priestly prayer of Jesus: "Holy Father, you have given me your name; now protect them by the power of your name so that they will be united just as we are" (John 17:11).

ENGAGE

☆ **Engage with other Jesus-followers in a lifestyle of prayer:** Visit nationalprayeraccord.com and see how you can be involved in this unified prayer rhythm. Then look for ways to pray with pastors and believers from other tribes.

SPIRIT-EMPOWERED *Faith*

Love the Lord L-2:
Spirit-empowered disciples love the Lord through listening to and hearing God for direction and discernment.

DAY 6

Be the Answer
Unity of Faith and Works

Our nation is facing a spiritual crisis.

The moment you separate body and spirit, the result is a corpse. Separate faith and works, and you get the same thing—a corpse. When there is a seamless unity of "believing and doing," we are exercising faith as God intends.

Much joy comes in our prayers as we listen to God's urging to "be the answer," trusting Him to show us how to meet the needs of those for whom we pray. At times, we may be a source of financial provision. This may be as simple as bringing a meal that's needed, offering words of encouragement, or going to the hospital to pray while someone is having surgery.

Our praying for others is vital and important; however, if we don't pair this with listening and responding to the voice of the Father, urging us to become the answer to the prayers, then we are only going halfway in our faith. When the burden is placed upon you to pray, God often will also give you a burden to respond. What a privilege that God chooses to work through His people to be the answer to their own prayers. When we respond in obedience, we learn what it truly means to be part of the body of Christ Jesus, and that is life-changing and culture-transforming.

THANKS

☆ *Give thanks to the Father:* Thank you, Father, for the privilege to colabor with you in behalf of the gospel as you unite my prayer and my walk.

CONFESSION

☆ *Listen for the Holy Spirit's prompting for confession:* We have often been prayerless in the face of crisis; forgive us. I have sadly, at times, only prayed while looking for others to fulfill my prayers; forgive me.

PETITION

☆ *Join Jesus in prayers of petition:* Holy Spirit, I yield myself to your authority and purpose, for "there is no authority except that which God has established" (Romans 13:1 NIV).

WORD

☆ *Proclaim promises from His Word:* Lord Jesus, might my prayerful walk with you be consistent with your Word as "a lamp to guide my feet and a light for my path" (Psalm 119:105).

ENGAGE

☆ **Engage with other Jesus-followers in a lifestyle of prayer:** Visit momsinprayer.org to discover ways to join others in passionately praying before God for the lives of our children. Imagine the impact of God answering prayers for a generation of children throughout the nation.

> **Love the Lord L-3:**
> Spirit-empowered disciples love the Lord through experiencing God as He really is through deepened intimacy with Him.

DAY 7

Extraordinary United Prayer

How good and pleasant it is
when God's people live together in unity!
PSALM 133:1 NIV

Have you ever wondered what makes the difference between a spotlight and a laser? How can a moderate laser burn through heavy metal in a matter of seconds, while the most powerful spotlight only makes it warm? Both may have similar electrical power, but the difference is in unity. All the laser photons (light beams) are in unison, and the spotlight photons move in all different directions.

In Scripture, we see both negative and positive examples of the power of unity. In Genesis 11, for example, when the whole world had one language and a common speech, they devised a plan to build for themselves a city with a tower reaching to the sky. The problem seems to be found in their motivation: "This will make us famous and keep us from being scattered all over the world" (Genesis 11:4).

This drew the Lord's attention. "Look!" he said. "The

people are united, and they all speak the same language. After this, nothing they set out to do will be impossible for them!" (Genesis 11:6). Of course, the result was a confusing of their language and a scattering of the people, thus stopping the building of the city.

Conversely, in Acts 2, on the day of Pentecost, when believers were all with one mind in the same place, they experienced a powerful visitation and infilling of the Holy Spirit (see Acts 2:1–4). This unifying force began to remove language, cultural, and national barriers, resulting in the salvation of three thousand souls. The synergy of their Spirit-empowered prayers created an extraordinary unity described in this way:

> And day by day, continuing steadfastly with one accord in the temple, and breaking bread at home, they took their food with gladness and singleness of heart, praising God, and having favor with all the people. And the Lord added to them day by day those that were saved. (Acts 2:46–47 ASV)

Drawing from both physical and spiritual illustrations, can you imagine what will transpire in our nation when God's people gather together in extraordinary united prayer? With laser-focused prayers, putting aside cultural, denominational, racial, generational, gender, and any other biases, we can ask God for a Christ awakening in our nation, and nothing will be impossible or withheld.

THANKS

☆ **Give thanks to the Father:** Father, we are grateful for the blessings you give those who walk in unity of spirit and purpose to glorify your name.

CONFESSION

☆ **Listen for the Holy Spirit's prompting for confession:** Forgive us that we have too often pursued those things which will make us renowned or favored in the public eye, and this has often divided and separated us from one another. Help us to remember Paul's encouragement to "do nothing out of selfish ambition or vain conceit. Rather, in humility value others above yourselves, not looking to your own interests but each of you to the interests of the others" (Philippians 2:3–4 NIV).

PETITION

☆ *Join Jesus in prayers of petition:* Help your people to live in such a way that we sense you saying, "This is good and pleasant," and experience the anointed power of prayer that comes when we are in unity, desiring to please you above all others, even ourselves.

WORD

☆ *Proclaim promises from His Word:* Father, as we walk in a love relationship with you and one another, we believe and proclaim that we will experience the answer to Christ's prayer: "May they experience such perfect unity that the world will know that you sent me and that you love them as much as you love me" (John 17:23).

ENGAGE

☆ **Engage with other Jesus-followers in a lifestyle of prayer:** Visit Intercessors for America at ifapray.org. They provide dynamic prayer guides to help synergize your prayers with others and action strategies to unite those throughout the nation who are praying for the restoration of godly values in our government, church, marketplace, and every arena of society. Visit ifapray. org to download your free guides and sign up to pray for our elected officials.

Love the Lord L-8:

Spirit-empowered disciples love the Lord through disciplined, bold, and believing prayer.

DAY 8

Revival Signs

*Our nation's greatest need is the
next great spiritual awakening.*

Look at any spiritual awakening in history, and you'll discover an obvious, common thread: Revival is always preceded by spiritual deadness. In the dry seasons of the church, there may be outward signs of life but the spiritual hearts of the people have stopped beating. This does not make the dry seasons any less a part of revival, however. God is still sovereign; He is still in charge. The dryness is just as much a part of the awakening as the prayers themselves. What other markers of revival can we trace? What other signs of revival mark our way? Here are just a few.

THE PRINCIPLE OF FULLNESS OF TIME

As it continues in all its "fullness," dryness always leads to desperation. Out of a profound sense of dissatisfaction, often with a certain degree of gloom, people begin to cry out to God. Remember the story of the Hebrides Islands in the late 1940s? A small group of men meeting in a barn began to cry out, "Oh, God, move on your people." Two women, down the road in a neighboring village, began to pray, "Oh, God, move." They cried out because there was nowhere else to turn. Their dryness led to desperation.

The story of the Hebrides is the story of virtually every revival: Out of a remnant, a large-scale movement is born, a movement that encompasses a large area. And often, strangely enough, the spiritual phenomenon that unfolds is largely unknown. Regardless of how anonymous God's hand is, revival occurs in "the fullness of time." His people in His time live out a principle of patience and faith in which the longings of God's followers are fully expressed.

THE PRINCIPLE OF BROKENNESS AND CONFESSION

Brokenness and confession is what the Holy Spirit brings and what the participants in revival experience. When brokenness, confession, and repentance begin to occur among God's people, revival spreads with extraordinary swiftness. As every revival in history bears out, individuals and the church as a whole wake up to the seriousness of their own sin. At times, the remorse can be overwhelming. People become concerned about the open sins of the flesh and the secret sins of the spirit. The greatest brokenness occurs in the life of believers as they come to grips with their own lack of love, and typically, the result is open and honest confession.

The principle of brokenness and confession yields to a wonderful outcome. As a result of confession and purification of the heart, people become so magnetically attracted to Christ that their dedication grows into a great enthusiasm to follow Him. Naturally, the good news is too life changing, too wonderful to contain. There's an enthusiasm to serve Jesus and a desire to bring others to Him. The person who experiences this new life in God wants everyone to know the one behind this new reality. This is evangelism in its most contagious form.

THANKS

☆ *Give thanks to the Father:* Bless you, Father, that you are attentive to the prayers of your people. Lord, I cry out to you today for a powerful revival. Sensitize my heart so that I am free to share my life with others. Thank you that you will empower me to share your good news with them too. Without your presence, there is no hope for a spiritual awakening. I ask that you rend the heavens and come down. I praise you for your presence that will flood our hearts and our lives in powerful ways.

CONFESSION

☆ *Listen for the Holy Spirit's prompting for confession:* "O Lord, I pray, open his eyes that he may see" (2 Kings

6:17 NASB). Pause now and pray the powerful prayer of Elisha. Listen for the Spirit's conviction concerning weakness of faith, fading hope, and spiritual blindness.

☆ Lord, I pray, open the eyes of your servants that they may see that those who are with us are more than those who are with them. Lord, open my eyes to a remnant of people who are asking you for revival and awakening despite the "dryness" of our time. Lord, by your Spirit, please give me the diligence to persevere in prayer. Encourage my hope for awakening through the prevailing prayers of others.

PETITION

☆ *Join Jesus in prayers of petition:* "I am humble and gentle …" (Matthew 11:29). Pause to meditate on the image of Jesus, the one who spoke these words. Imagine that Christ stands before you. He has heard your prayers for revival. He has seen your sadness and confusion over the desperate places of our world. Now imagine His response. The Savior doesn't offer you a lecture. He doesn't look at you sternly or with indifference. Instead, the one person who can bring revival and who can direct our steps toward awakening makes this declaration: "Come to me. I am here for you as your humble and gentle teacher."

☆ Spend a few moments now, asking for the Spirit's work of Christlikeness in your own life—particularly for His work of humility. Ask the Lord to make this change so that you will be available for all He may desire. Lord, deepen your work of humility in me. I want to be humble and gentle just like you. I want to be teachable and available just like you. Involve me in your move of spiritual awakening in whatever ways you desire.

WORD

☆ ***Proclaim promises from His Word:*** "We loved you so much that we shared with you not only God's Good News but our own lives, too" (1 Thessalonians 2:8). Consider praying this prayer with another follower of Jesus. Ask the Lord to empower you to share both your life and the good news with others: Lord, I ask you to help me share my life with others. Help me convey both my love and your love. Give us such a passion for sharing our lives and the gospel that a movement begins in our community.

ENGAGE

☆ **Engage with other Jesus-followers in a lifestyle of prayer:** Ask the Holy Spirit to reveal one specific person who could benefit from your investment of time, of care, and of your life. Who needs the gospel shared through your life? Lord, show me the person who needs me to share life with them. Who needs your gospel? Show me, Lord, for I'm listening. Visit thecenterforawakening.com.

Love the Lord L-5:
Spirit-empowered disciples love the Lord through living with a passionate longing for purity and to please Him in all things.

DAY 9

Turning a Nation to God

Beyond all things put on love,
which is the perfect bond of unity.

COLOSSIANS 3:14 ESV

Our nation is in serious trouble. From sea to shining sea, we are witnessing the devolution of a nation. The United States is quickly becoming the divided states, as signs of disunity and conflicts abound. From family breakdowns, to the immigration crisis, to the abiding racial divide, to Congress' inability to function, it is clear we are a fraying nation. Add to this the continuing moral decay that is engulfing us, whether it is the redefinition of marriage and the family, abortions on demand, a media that continues to dumb down decency, or an educational system that increasingly seeks to impart information without ethics in the name of "freedom."

We are as a nation sliding south. But there is a way back. We can return to our roots by a wholehearted pleading of the people of God through repentance and prayer. When we respond in this way, then God will hear our cry, see our hearts, and turn and heal our land. God and His rule is our nation's only hope; and the church operating under His authority is the means for the realization of that hope, since it alone has been given the keys of the kingdom (see Matthew 16:18–19).

A DECLARATION OF DEPENDENCE

Since national revival begins with Christians comprehensively functioning under God's rule, it is time for a new declaration. America was born out of a desire for independence from the tyranny of England. But spiritual revival demands just the opposite. It requires verbal and visible dependence on God. If we want God to bless America, then America must first bless God. This means His people must first totally dedicate allegiance to Him through the four covenantal kingdom spheres

He has established. Those four spheres are personal, familial, the church, and national.

A PERSONAL DECLARATION OF DEPENDENCE

Every Christian must decide to no longer serve two masters. God makes it clear that we cannot have the world and have Him at the same time (see 1 John 2:15–17). Each day must begin with a commitment to Him above all else, and He is to be consulted in prayer on all matters of life (see Luke 9:23).

A FAMILY DECLARATION OF DEPENDENCE

"As for me and my house, we will serve the LORD" (Joshua 24:15). The dinner table must again become the central place for reviewing and applying kingdom principles (see Psalm 128:3). Couples must reconnect themselves to their biblical roles and hate divorce as much as God does (see Malachi 2:14).

THE CHURCH'S DECLARATION OF DEPENDENCE

Local churches must recommit themselves to their primary responsibility of making disciples and not be satisfied with simply expanding their membership. Jesus doesn't need more fans. He wants more followers. In addition, there must be a radical return by church leadership to the authority of Scripture and the priority of prayer as the foundation of church life (see 1 Timothy 2:8–9). The church must have regular, unified sacred gatherings to keep the focus on our absolute dependency on God.

A NATIONAL DECLARATION OF DEPENDENCE

The church must again become the conscience of the government. Through its national solemn assembly, it should clearly and respectfully call political leaders to God's principles for government (see Romans 13:1–7), which means we cannot be so entrenched with political parties that we are not free to speak truth to those in power. *It also means we must begin speaking with one voice, so the nation sees a unified church and not one divided by faith.*

In addition, we should so overwhelm the culture with good works that the benefit we bring cannot be overlooked or denied (see Matthew 5:16). Finally, all attempts to remove God from the marketplace ought to be resisted while we simultaneously bring our public officials in prayer before the throne of grace (see 1 Timothy 2:1–3).

As God's kingdom agenda is manifested simultaneously through His four covenantal spheres, in a spirit of dependence on Him, then we will have done our part in welcoming the glory of our great God to be among us and for God to bring the revival we and our nation so desperately need, before it's too late.

THANKS

☆ **Give thanks to the Father:** Thanks, Lord, that you hear me when I cry out to you to bring our country back to you. I am depending upon you to change me and reveal yourself to others through me. I praise you that you can use me for your glory. Empower me by your Spirit. Cause my heart to be awakened toward you and fill me with a passion to serve you.

CONFESSION

☆ **Listen for the Holy Spirit's prompting for confession:** "So now, come back to your God. Act with love and justice, and always depend on him" (Hosea 12:6). Stop and reflect on your personal relationship with the Lord and your family relationships for a few moments. Ask the Holy Spirit to assess these specific areas of your life. Ask Him to show you if you have strayed from His purposes and His desires and need to return. Declare your dependence upon Him: God, is there any area of my personal life or family life where I am not allowing you to be Lord? Search me and show me any areas where I have strayed and need to come back to you.

☆ Pause until the Holy Spirit speaks to you. Then make this declaration: Lord, I declare my dependence upon you. I need your help to change, and I need your power to act differently, especially in the area of _____.

PETITION

☆ ***Join Jesus in prayers of petition:*** "For apart from me you can do nothing" (John 15:5). None of us as individuals, families, or His church has any hope of living an abundant life in our own strength. Take a moment and imagine yourself bowing before the Lord as He reminds you: "Your energy, your creativity, your strength, and your intellect are all provisions from me. You are wonderfully made, but remember that apart from Me you can do absolutely nothing."

☆ As you bow before the Lord, make a declaration of your helplessness, a declaration of your dependence upon God, and an acknowledgement of your hope in Him: Lord, my power and strength are insufficient for all that I face in this world—I need you. Restore my perspective. I know I am nothing without you, but I know you are with me, available for me, and sufficient for all my needs. I turn to you now.

WORD

☆ ***Proclaim promises from His Word:*** "… Christ in you, the hope of glory" (Colossians 1:27 NASB). Consider for a moment how God sees you as a bearer of His glory for your family, friends, community, and nation. How does this impact your heart? "When I reflect on the truth that Christ is in me and I get to reveal His glory, I feel _____."

☆ Plan to share your reflections with a friend, family member, or small group: "I want to do my part to reveal God's glory—to show the incredible power of Jesus Christ in the world in which I live. He's recently shown me how I need to change _____ so that I can be a better representation of Him."

ENGAGE

☆ **Engage with other Jesus-followers in a lifestyle of prayer:** Ask the Holy Spirit to show you ways in which you can reach out and do your part to overwhelm your community with good works. How will you serve the "least of these" in your neighborhood?

☆ Holy Spirit, show me how I can "do good" for the people in my community who need it the most. Give me creative ideas and practical applications for how to best love the people you have placed me around. Help me to point others to you as I serve them with the love you have shed abroad in my heart. Visit missionamerica.org.

Love the Lord L-10:
Spirit-empowered disciples love the Lord, practicing the presence of the Lord, yielding to Spirit's work of Christlikeness.

DAY 10

Preserve the Unity of the Spirit

Our nation is facing a Holy Spirit crisis.

May our desire to experience more of the Holy Spirit be our starting point, not our endgame. And may we open our hearts and lives to His presence and action more fully than we have ever done before.

By the power and presence of the Holy Spirit, we can be a people who live a life of transformation and power, a life that clearly points to the one who deserves all of our praise. It is by the power of the Holy Spirit that we are progressively made into the image and likeness of Christ, and it is by His might that we are empowered to live the life Jesus called us to live.

There is a big gap between what we read in Scripture about the Holy Spirit and how most believers and churches operate today. In many modern churches, we would be stunned by the apparent absence of the Spirit in any manifest way. The missing *something* in our church experience is actually a missing *someone*—namely, the Holy Spirit. Without Him, people operate in their own strength and only accomplish human-sized results. The world is not moved by love or actions that are of human creation. And the church is not empowered to live differently from any other gathering of people without the Holy Spirit. But when believers live in the power of the Spirit, the evidence in their lives is supernatural.

The church cannot help but be different, and the world cannot help but notice: "The members of the council were amazed when they saw the boldness of Peter and John, for they could see that they were ordinary men with no special training in the Scriptures. They also recognized them as men who had been with Jesus" (Acts 4:13).

Some people talk a lot about—even boast of—the Spirit, but their lives do not bear His fruit. Others speak of the Holy Spirit in theoretical or scholarly terms yet do not experience Him at work. Still others ignore Him for all practical purposes and, as you might expect, rarely experience relationship or intimacy with the Spirit. And then there is that rare person who doesn't talk frequently about the Spirit, yet whose life is a powerful display of His presence and activity.

As believers, we can never be "done" with God. He is infinite and we are finite; there will always be more of His character to discover, more of His love to experience, and more of His power to use for His purposes.

THANKS

☆ ***Give thanks to the Father:*** I praise you, Father, that I don't have to settle for the closeness I have with you now. I know there's more—a lot more. Thank you that I can have more of your Spirit's closeness, more intimacy with you, more Christlike transformation, and more power in my life. I'm crying out for more of you, Jesus, for I know there is so much more to be received.

CONFESSION

☆ ***Listen for the Holy Spirit's prompting for confession:***
Let God transform you into a new person (see Romans
12:2). Pause for a moment and ask the Holy Spirit to
show you an area of your life that needs His transformation—specifically, a change that is needed that will
only be explained by the work and presence of the
Spirit of God. Ask God's Spirit to make such a change
in you that others can't help but recognize that you
have been with Jesus: Holy Spirit, what part of my life
needs to change today? What part of my life needs to
change in such a way that people around me can't help
but notice? Show me, Lord. And then empower that
change within me. I want to be a beacon of transformation that points others to you.

PETITION

☆ ***Join Jesus in prayers of petition:*** "But I will send you
the Advocate—the Spirit of truth. He will come to you
from the Father and will testify all about me" (John
15:26). Ask the Holy Spirit to be your Advocate today.
Ask Him to reveal more of Jesus as you reflect on the
needs of your life and the circumstances of your world.

☆ Now ask the Holy Spirit to testify about the unity of the
Spirit that is found in Jesus. Does the Spirit want you
to know that Jesus is the all-powerful one, the Mighty
Counselor, the Great I Am, the Prince of Peace, the
Great Provider, the Attentive One, the Gracious One, or
the Great Physician? One of the Spirit's jobs is to reveal
more of Jesus.

☆ Holy Spirit, given the needs of my life and the challenges of my world, what do you want to testify about
Jesus? How might you want me to better live out the
unity of my faith with others? Listen as the Spirit testi-
fies more about Him.

WORD

☆ ***Proclaim promises from His Word:*** "By this all men will know that you are My disciples if you have love for one another" (John 13:35 NASB). Lord, speak to me about a time when you were longing for me to share your love with others.

> o I could have listened more to _____, but I missed the opportunity.
>
> o I could have apologized to _____, but I didn't.
>
> o I could have helped more, but instead I _____.
>
> o And I could have shared more appreciation, but instead I _____.

☆ As the Holy Spirit speaks to you, offer a humble prayer: Lord, I want others to see the evidence of the work of your Spirit in my life. I regret the times when I have missed your prompting. Make me more sensitive to your voice, empower my actions, and deepen my unity with your people.

ENGAGE

☆ **Engage with other Jesus-followers in a lifestyle of prayer:** "… wherever the Spirit of the Lord is, there is freedom" (2 Corinthians 3:17). Tell someone your story about the times when you have experienced the presence of the Holy Spirit in your life. The times where you have experienced freedom and change mean that these are the times you have surrendered, and the Spirit of the Lord was present to work within you. Talk also about the additional areas of freedom and change that are still needed. Then spend some time praying together: Holy Spirit, I want more and more of your freedom in my life, especially in the area of _____. Show me what I need to surrender to you. I want to see and sense the Spirit of the Lord in my life in a real and powerful way. Visit globaloutreachday.com.

Love the Lord L-9:
Spirit-empowered disciples love the Lord through yielding to the Spirit's fullness as life in the Spirit brings supernatural intimacy with the Lord, manifestations of divine gifts, and witness of the fruit of the Spirit.

DAY 11

Prayer for Our Nation's Leaders

Our nation is facing a leadership crisis.

P aul wrote, "First of all then, I urge that petitions, prayers, intercessions, and thanksgivings be made for everyone, for kings and all those who are in authority, so that we may lead a tranquil and quiet life in all godliness and dignity" (1 Timothy 2:1–2 HCSB). Imagine what could happen if thousands across our nation and the world would unite in prayer for the nation with the same prayer priorities, beginning with prayer for our leaders.

The political and societal landscape of our communities can often look hopeless. It's not hard to find fault with many of our leaders. But how should we respond? How can we position ourselves as intercessors for the leaders we may never meet? The story of Daniel provides a perfect example.

Daniel served his country valiantly. Even his enemies determined that Daniel was completely trustworthy. Consequently, the only grounds of accusation they could find were related to Daniel's religion. His enemies executed a wicked scheme, and Daniel found himself in a den of lions because of his faithfulness to the living God.

Daniel's life angered most of the political leaders, but the king's response tells us that Daniel's integrity did not go unnoticed. Having observed Daniel's life of integrity and commitment to His God, the king hoped that Daniel's life was spared. One man's example of living faith turned the heart of a king.

Thousands of years ago, Jesus confirmed the truth of our day: "The world's sin is that it refuses to believe in me" (John 16:9). Many of our leaders refuse to believe in Jesus. So how do we now pray? First, we must live a life of integrity and commitment to our God. And then we pray Christ's prayer in John 16. We rest assured that "when he comes, he will convict the world of its sin, and of God's righteousness" (John 16:8). We pray that the Holy Spirit would convict hearts and point our leaders to the one true God as we live as modern-day Daniels, living so that our faith will turn the hearts of kings.

THANKS

☆ **Give thanks to the Father:** Heavenly Father, I offer my thanks and praise that you have chosen me for divine purpose and mission. I rejoice in your sovereignty over every leader in our nation. May your kingdom come and your will be done on earth as it is in heaven.

CONFESSION

☆ **Listen for the Holy Spirit's prompting for confession:** Search me, Lord; remove from my life everything that distracts from my kingdom witness. Refine me, change me, and engage me as salt and light in a dark world.

☆ Pause for a moment and ask the Holy Spirit to show you an area of your life that needs His transformation—specifically, a change that will only be explained by the work and presence of the Spirit of God. Ask God's Spirit to make such a change in you that others can't help but recognize you have been with Jesus.

PETITION

☆ **Join Jesus in prayers of petition:** Lord Jesus, we appeal to you for our president, vice president, cabinet members, and members of both the House and Senate to make decisions that will lead toward a more peaceful and orderly America. Lord, we also ask that these leaders lead us to ways better representing you and your ways; including decisions leading toward the dignity and sanctity of all human life from conception until natural death. Lord God, may these leaders provide ways for our nation to be secure from terrorism inside and outside our nation's borders.

WORD

☆ ***Proclaim promises from His Word:*** "Each of you should use whatever gift you have received to serve others, as faithful stewards of God's grace in its various forms" (1 Peter 4:10 NIV). Pause to ask the Lord how He might want you to be different from the people of the world. Does God want you to be more patient, kind, joyful, peaceful, faithful, gentle, loving, or self-controlled? Ask Jesus to reveal His desire specifically for you.

☆ Lord, because of your sacrifice for me, I want my life to look different from the people who don't know you as their Savior. How do you want my life to be different? Who needs to see this demonstration of the fruit of the Spirit in my life?

ENGAGE

☆ **Engage with other Jesus-followers in a lifestyle of prayer:** Visit cpcfoundation.com to support the work of the Congressional Prayer Caucus.

Love People P-1:
Spirit-empowered disciples love people through living a Spirit-led life of doing good in all of life: relationships and vocation, community and calling.

DAY 12

How to Pray for Your Pastor

"Call to Me and I will answer you, and I will tell you great and mighty things, which you do not know."

JEREMIAH 33:3 NASB

Every Christ-follower engaged in a local church has a pastor. These followers of Christ should pray for their pastors. Pastors may appear as though they are so strong that they do not need prayer, but be assured, any pastor genuinely called to the ministry knows he needs prayer—earnest, passionate, and effective prayer. "Pray for me" should be the number-one personal request from a pastor of the church he serves.

STAND ON GOD'S WORD WHEN YOU PRAY FOR YOUR PASTOR

The strength of prayer stands on the authority of Holy Scripture. You need to stand on the infallibility and truthfulness of God's Word when you pray for your pastor. Paul was praying this for the believers in Colossae, and these words can be prayed for your pastor too:

> For this reason also, since the day we heard this, we haven't stopped praying for you. We are asking that you may be filled with the knowledge of His will in all wisdom and spiritual understanding, so that you may walk worthy of the Lord, fully pleasing to Him, bearing fruit in every good work and growing in the knowledge of God. May you be strengthened with all power, according to His glorious might, so that you may have endurance and patience, with joy giving thanks to the Father, who has enabled you to share in the saints' inheritance in the light. (Colossians 1:9–12 HCSB)

Here are five specific ways to pray for your pastor.

THANKS

☆ ***Give thanks to the Father:*** Heavenly Father, thank you that my pastor can be filled with the knowledge of your will.

☆ Pastors face the same dilemma people faced in the first century, when these words were penned. The knowledge of the world pours into the minds of pastors, but pastors need to have the full knowledge of God's will. The will of God does not inflate a pastor's ego, but it enlightens us to do what God wills for us to do.

☆ Father, thank you that you will give my pastor the full knowledge of your will in all things at all times, personally and for our church.

CONFESSION

☆ ***Listen for the Holy Spirit's prompting for confession:*** Lord, I pray my pastor will turn from anything that hinders being filled with all spiritual wisdom.

☆ Pastors will view life from one of two perspectives: the world or the Spirit. Only the Holy Spirit will always lead a pastor to the Word of God and the will of God. The Spirit of God will lead a pastor to view life and ministry from God's perspective, not his own. His perspective will determine his decision-making.

☆ Holy Spirit, fill my pastor with your wisdom and perspective about all things in his life, in our church, and in this world.

PETITION

☆ ***Join Jesus in prayers of petition:*** Lord Jesus, fill my pastor with spiritual understanding that will help him put facts and information together biblically, spiritually, and practically.

WORD

☆ ***Proclaim promises from His Word:*** "We have not ceased to pray for you … so that you will walk in a manner worthy of the Lord" (Colossians 1:9–10 NASB). Oh Lord, empower my pastor to walk in a way that would exemplify you to all persons, pleasing you in all ways, and bearing fruit in every way before others.

ENGAGE

☆ **Engage with other Jesus-followers in supporting your pastor:** Pastors should be full of spiritual vitality. They need the spiritual strength to overcome the challenges of each day in ministry. Submission to God daily will lead to God's power. This power is so strong that a pastor is able to endure stress and suffering that ministry brings. It is so powerful that he will refuse to retaliate in any way toward difficult people and circumstances. It is even so strong that he will live life and do ministry with true joy that overflows with thanksgiving to God. Every pastor needs this kind of power.

☆ Join with others in establishing a pastor prayer team in your local church beginning with just seven people (or couples) who will commit to lifting their pastor and family one day each week. Visit care4pastors.com to download information on this strategy and supportive resources.

☆ Oh God, enlist some of your saints to help strengthen my pastor with your power that fills him with spiritual life daily, including the difficult days of life and ministry, and lead him to persevere with joy and thanksgiving.

SPIRIT-EMPOWERED *Faith*

Love People P-3:
Spirit-empowered disciples love people through discerning the relational needs of others with a heart to give of His love.

DAY 13

Prayers for Arts and Media

Righteousness exalts a nation,
but sin is a disgrace to any people.
PROVERBS 14:34 HCSB

Every day, the world's value system bombards us through the news, television, and movies. We are impacted by time spent listening to music, playing video games, and browsing or engaging the Internet. Magazines and tabloids "jump off" the store racks at us. While it's irresponsible to blame all our culture's problems on the media, there is a dark side that draws most of us into its web, whether it's emotional, sexual, intellectual, spiritual, or physical.

We need to pray first for ourselves, that we would acknowledge the battle being fought for our hearts, minds, and souls. Then we need to ask God for wisdom and discernment to see through the unhealthy entertainment choices we are making for ourselves and for our children.

Far too few of us realize how much our media and entertainment-focused culture influences us and our families—morally, spiritually, and ethically. Let's pray that His Spirit would bring the refiner's fire and purity, so those who profess His name would represent Him well.

Our nation's vast media and entertainment industries do much to shape the minds of our people every single day. They shape the opinions of both leaders and followers. They reach into the lives of the old, middle-aged, and young alike. Every day, across our nation, we open our minds to hours and hours of "influence."

From newspapers, to television, to radio, to websites, to apps for everything, we receive a steady stream of input daily.

From Facebook, to Twitter, to Snapchat, to YouTube, we spend large portions of our week reading, watching, and listening to media and entertainment of every kind.

Like no other generation, we spend much of our free time allowing movies, television programming, news, and advertising—both good and bad, both positive and negative—to flow freely through our minds. What we put into our minds influences what we think and how we feel. Watch a sad movie and you'll probably cry. Watch a comedy and you'll most likely laugh. Watch a scary movie and you'll experience fear.

The enemy of our souls can use this powerful emotional connection as a form of manipulation and as an opportunity to misdirect us away from "what is true, and honorable, and right, and pure, and lovely, and admirable" when we should be pursuing those things that are "excellent and worthy of praise" (Philippians 4:8).

PRAY, EXPECTING TRANSFORMATION

The media is unquestionably one of the most powerful and influential voices in our culture. Let's ask the Lord to provide the television, radio, and print mediums with staff members and executives who are committed to accuracy and integrity. We must also remember to intercede on behalf of the artists, actors, musicians, and athletes our young people seek to emulate.

THANKS

☆ ***Give thanks to the Father:*** Lord, we praise you that every day, thousands of Christians from coast to coast work in the arena of secular media and entertainment, trying to be salt and light in what are often difficult and challenging workplaces. I ask you to raise up godly men and women who are extraordinarily gifted to bring change and goodness to the media and entertainment arena in which they work.

CONFESSION

☆ *Listen for the Holy Spirit's prompting for confession:* Though the media bears responsibility for the entertainment they present, my choices do not always reflect my love for you and your principles. I ask you to show me if there are areas of my life or areas of my family's life where I am allowing unhealthy influences and messages. Holy Spirit, help me to take a stand for what is right and to repent of any sin.

PETITION

☆ *Join Jesus in prayers of petition:* "Walk in the light while you can, so the darkness will not overtake you" (John 12:35). I pray that journalists across our nation will do their best to bring light where there is darkness and truth where there is deception. Father, strengthen and direct the will of the writers and shape the coverage of newspapers, television, radio, and magazines. Please remove those who desire to report anything less than the truth and are not a service to humanity. May you raise up those who are bold to confront evil and injustice, who reject the half-truths that deceive and the biased words that corrupt. I ask you to promote those who will use the power of their words for good and bring the respect and integrity of character that honors their profession. Give wisdom, honesty, and courage to those who seek your face and restore a righteous standard of journalism, so truth might prevail throughout our nation.

WORD

☆ *Proclaim promises from His Word:* "Saul! Saul! Why are you persecuting me?" (Acts 9:4). Miracles still happen and God is still the same. Pray for producers, directors, writers, and studio executives of television shows and motion pictures. Lord, work in miraculous ways to win their hearts and minds to the gospel. I pray for those who create video games, those who write and sing music, for actors and celebrities, and for those who develop the content for websites. May you shine the light of truth into their hearts and bring conviction of sin that leads to repentance and righteousness. Jesus, show yourself to them as you did to Saul of Tarsus on the road to Damascus, and raise up a generation of godly men and women in the entertainment world who will be true to your Word. I trust you to bring your truth and salvation to them and set them free to be a powerful force for good.

ENGAGE

☆ **Engage with other Jesus-followers in a life-style of prayer:** The Hollywood Prayer Network is a global prayer network, led by entertainment-industry Christians, seeking to impact our culture for Christ through prayer. Visit hollywoodprayernetwork.org to become engaged in interceding for the world's most influential mission field. Movieguide .org provides movie and television reviews from a faith and family perspective.

Love People P-9:
Spirit-empowered disciples demonstrate His love to an ever-growing network of other people, as He continues to challenge us to love beyond our comfort.

DAY 14

Pray for Our Military

There is no greater love than to lay down one's life for one's friends.
JOHN 15:13

Courage, sacrifice, and service would be among numerous affirmations we could bestow on our military men and women and their families. It seems only appropriate that we should serve, through our fervent intercession, those who have served us, whether they are in active duty or veterans. We are privileged to approach the throne of grace on behalf of these servants as we:

1. Mobilize intercessors for those who are in authority (see 1 Timothy 2:1–4).
2. Engage men and women who are willing to stand in the gap on behalf of the land, so He will not destroy it (see Ezekiel 22:30; 2 Chronicles 7:13–14).
3. Thank God for these men and women who, like King David, release God's blessings and favor on their people because they boldly worship God and acknowledge His sovereignty (see 1 Chronicles 29:10–13).
4. Believe God will position people in the military who love justice and hate injustice so that it will be evident to all people why our nation and others like it are blessed (see Isaiah 61:8–9).
5. Ask God to position righteous people in these leadership roles so His people may thrive and rejoice (see Proverbs 29:2).
6. Intercede that God will raise up leaders who, like Cyrus, can fulfill the word of God, to restore ruins and rebuild cities, and to establish God's community within a region or territory (see Isaiah 44:28).
7. Beseech God to engage anointed leaders who have the skills and authority to subdue rulers and nations who act wrongly toward God's children (see 2 Samuel 22:32–51; Isaiah 45:1).

As we intercede for these men and women to walk in the fear of the Lord and revere God's Word, He will prepare and equip them to be sensitive to the needs of all people and have great wisdom to know how to meet those needs. God desires to engage people like Joseph who will have the wisdom, knowledge, and understanding to protect and provide for nations in seasons of distress (see Genesis 41).

Imagine the impact our military would have if, like Daniel and his compatriots, they were equipped with godly wisdom, knowledge, and courage to confound nations living in the darkness of false religion and ideology (see Daniel 1:17–20). We can be encouraged to know as we intercede that God will release a spirit of justice and righteousness to restrain evil in our world.

THANKS

☆ *Give thanks to the Father:* Thank God for men and women in these areas of leadership who, like King Solomon, have great wisdom and knowledge and, by their courage and favor, release blessings on the people (see 2 Chronicles 1:12).

CONFESSION

☆ *Listen for the Holy Spirit's prompting for confession:* Pray for these leaders to be humble, committed to their comrades, and even to lay their lives down on behalf of our nation as Moses did for Israel (see James 4:6; Exodus 32). And then listen as His Spirit may speak to you about humility, commitment to others, and willingness to sacrifice. Change me, Lord.

PETITION

☆ *Join Jesus in prayers of petition:* We ask you, Father, to continue raising up these men and women as leaders who serve the people with justice under the fear of the Lord (see 2 Samuel 23:3). We also ask, Lord, that you would protect the spouses and children of those who serve us courageously.

WORD

☆ ***Proclaim promises from His Word:*** "But the Lord is faithful; He will strengthen you and guard you from the evil one" (2 Thessalonians 3:3). Lord, we claim your protection over these, for you are the Faithful One with whom nothing is impossible.

ENGAGE

☆ **Engage with other Jesus-followers in supporting those who serve and protect:** Be intentional to engage with and serve military families in your church or community. Support specific military-oriented ministries that serve our service men and women and their families. Visit momsofmilitary.com to engage in prayer for our military and operationwearehere.com, which provides practical ideas for supporting military families, including downloadable thank-you cards.

Love People P-8:

Spirit-empowered disciples take courageous initiative as peacemakers, reconciling relationships along life's journey.

DAY 15

Prayer for Education

The fear of the LORD is the beginning of knowledge,
but fools despise wisdom and discipline.

PROVERBS 1:7 HCSB

In 1836, Noah Webster, often called "The Father of American Education," stated, "In my view, the Christian religion is the most important and one of the first things in which all children under a free government ought to be instructed .... No truth is more evident … than that the Christian religion must be the basis of any government intended to secure the rights and privileges of a free people."*

Throughout history, and still today, every person's life has been, or is being, impacted by those working in the field of education. We entrust our children and grandchildren into their hands every day. Shouldn't we be taking the time to pray individually for every teacher and administrator who is involved in our lives? Shouldn't we pray for our local school board members and district superintendents? Don't become discouraged! Continue to pray! The effective, fervent prayers that you offer up for them come with a promise from God—they will avail much!

It is especially critical that we pray for a restoration of godly teaching and morality in our nation's educational system. It has been estimated that there are more than 500,000 Christian teachers in public schools. The Spirit of God resides within them and is working through them as they live out their faith day by day—through caring interactions with students; through effective teaching that enables students to develop their unique, God-given gifts; through teaching commonly accepted values, such as honesty, respect, and caring for others; and through teaching about religion within the curriculum.

The psalmist asked, "When the foundations are being destroyed, what can the righteous do?" (Psalm 11:3 HCSB). Many people are surprised when they hear that most of America's oldest universities were started by preachers and churches—Harvard, William and Mary, Yale, Princeton, King's College, Brown, Rutgers, and Dartmouth. For example, Harvard University was founded in 1636 and adopted the "Rules and Precepts" that stated: "Let every student be plainly instructed, and earnestly pressed to consider well, the main end of his life and studies is, to know God and Jesus Christ which is eternal life, John 17:3, and therefore to lay Christ in the bottom, as the only foundation of all sound knowledge and learning."**

---

* Noah Webster, as cited by Kay Dee Lilley, *God's Country, America's Heartcry* (Maitland, FL: Xulon Press, 2010), 149.
** https://nccs.net/1997-10-the-founding-of-harvard-college.

By way of contrast, today's universities and colleges are citadels of moral relativism in which the notion of absolute right and wrong is nonexistent, and where research shows that 70 percent of students from "Christian" homes deny their faith before graduation. Together we can focus on praying specifically for:

1. Christian teachers to have a tremendous impact on the lives of their students and positively influence the cultures, values, and spiritual environments of their schools.
2. The Holy Spirit to use Christian professors and faculty members as a force for good and that a new standard might be raised within the sphere of education.
3. Christian students to stand strong for their faith and grow in profound ways.
4. The Lord to equip churches and homes across the land to give their young people the training for a biblical worldview that will cause them to thrive in their faith through their entire college experience.

We must be convinced our children are gifts from God who are worthy of our prayer and that He is able to do immeasurably more than we ask of Him.

THANKS

☆ *Give thanks to the Father:* Father in heaven, I thank you that so many of the Founding Fathers of our nation were so strong about the role of religion and morality in the shaping of our educational foundations. Bring a revival of godliness and a movement of the Holy Spirit among those who can influence and change harmful policies. We ask you for a miracle.

CONFESSION

☆ *Listen for the Holy Spirit's prompting for confession:* "Train up a child in the way he should go, and when he is old he will not depart from it" (Proverbs 22:6 NKJV).

☆ In Paula J. Fox's book, *The Heart of a Teacher*, she says to her fellow teachers: "A child's heart is fragile don't break it. A child's mind is open don't close it. A child's soul is tender don't harden it. A child's spirit is joyful don't crush it." Every child bears an originality that is evidence of the image of God in his or her life.

☆ Pause to listen for the Spirit's prompting related to your parenting and/or grandparenting and to your child's heart, mind, soul, and spirit. Change me, Lord, as you find areas of needed transformation, so I may better serve the children in my life.

PETITION

☆ *Join Jesus in prayers of petition:* Lord, I ask you to inspire all Christians in education to be your shining light in our schools. I pray that teachers and school administrative leaders would fear you and understand that they have a great responsibility as they train our nation's future leaders.

☆ Holy Spirit, fill the lives of teachers in our Christian schools and homeschools with your presence. And by their shining examples, I ask you to draw young people to follow Jesus.

WORD

☆ *Proclaim promises from His Word:* "Let your light so shine before men, that they may see your good works and glorify your Father in heaven" (Matthew 5:16 NKJV). I pray that Christian teachers will have a tremendous impact on the lives of their students and positively influence the cultures, values, and spiritual environments of their schools. Lord, I ask you to inspire all Christians in education to be your shining light in schools by being role models and mentors for the younger generations.

ENGAGE

☆ **Engage with other Jesus-followers in a lifestyle of prayer:** Christian Educators Association International encourages, equips, and empowers Christian educators to effectively walk out their calling in their schools. Access resources to answer common questions about religious freedom in schools, provide specific prayer targets, and offer membership with insurance and other benefits for educators. Not only can you engage in prayer, but you can also share this great ministry with educators with whom you intersect. Visit CEAI.org to learn more.

SPIRIT-EMPOWERED *Faith*

Love People P-2:
Spirit-empowered disciples startle people with loving initiatives to "give first."

DAY 16

Pray for Marketplace Leaders

The LORD detests dishonest scales,
but accurate weights find favor with him.
PROVERBS 11:1 NIV

The greatest platform God has given you is your *work*. Praying for Him to raise up godly business leaders is of critical importance. It's the marketplace that creates work and industry to provide honest employment and generous provision for individuals and families. Work is of sacred importance to the Creator, and the workplace is where Jesus-followers live out the life and love of Jesus.

As we are interceding for the marketplace, we must recognize that God's servants, who are walking in integrity, humility, faithfulness, and righteousness, are those who will be blessed with knowledge, wisdom, and understanding that comes from Him. In a dark world where truth and kindness may sometimes be rare commodities, they will shine as lights by being trustworthy, kindhearted, pure, discrete, and generous.

God's men and women in the marketplace must remember that the Lord their God is the one who gives them the ability to produce wealth; this is how He confirms His covenant, which He swore to our forefathers (see Deuteronomy 8:18). We cannot place a financial value on the knowledge of God's will, spiritual wisdom, and understanding, but those gifts are what enable marketplace leaders to live lives pleasing to the Lord, bearing fruit in every good work.

Not only are we blessed, but people throughout the nation will be blessed when God's servants commit all they do to the Lord so their plans will succeed (see Proverbs 16:3), honor the Lord with their wealth, with the firstfruits of all their labors (see Proverbs 3:9–10), and seek to build God's kingdom first and foremost, seeking to walk in God's righteousness so everything he or she needs will be provided (see Matthew 6:33).

THANKS

☆ **Give thanks to the Father:** We're thankful, Father, for the good things that you have given to us, including even the strength to "make wealth" (Deuteronomy 8:10) and bear fruit through the work of our hands.

CONFESSION

☆ **Listen for the Holy Spirit's prompting for confession:** Pause to consider your marketplace testimony. Are you being rich in good deeds, generous, and willing to share? Listen as the Holy Spirit speaks of changes in your stewardship, serving, and sharing (see 1 Timothy 6:11–18).

PETITION

☆ ***Join Jesus in prayers of petition:*** Jesus' desire is for His sons and daughters to be free from the love of money. Pray that God will help you to be content and fulfilled by the knowledge of His presence in your life (see 1 Timothy 6:6–10; Hebrew 13:5).

WORD

☆ ***Proclaim promises from His Word:*** "Give, and it will be given …" (Luke 6:38 NIV). Pray for those in the market-place to be generous as God is generous to them; ask for the Spirit's prompting in you to live generously.

ENGAGE

☆ Engage with other Jesus-followers in a lifestyle of prayer: Join with others in your community in praying for specific industries and businesses by name, asking for God's truth to be upheld and His blessings to be made evident. Consider MarketplaceLeaders.org and the Institute of Faith, Work, and Economics (tifwe.org) as excellent resources for biblical perspectives on the marketplace.

Love People P-10:
Spirit-empowered disciples humbly acknowledge to the Lord, ourselves, and others that it is Jesus, in and through us, who is loving others at their point of need.

DAY 17

Freedom, Faith, and Families

We stand believing that freedom of religion for all people promotes the common good of our nation and the world.

From the very beginning of our nation, America's Founders raised a bulwark against certain crimes. They set forth not only a vision of self-government but a conviction—a creed—that our freedoms are the unalienable gift of God. These freedoms can be assaulted or infringed, but they can never be erased because they are written, as Alexander Hamilton wrote, "by the hand of Divinity itself."

We must never become indifferent to what has been won at such incredible cost. We assert once more that we never will. The threats our nation faces are not potential—they are clear, present, and dangerous. On every measure from criminal activity, to educational achievement, to fidelity and happiness in marriage, to personal productivity and longevity, religious practices and intact family structures predict and produce the best results. The implications for government policy are profound: every dollar spent on a program to improve childhood education, reduce street crime, increase earnings, or spur invention is severely undercut by any government action that undermines family foundation and religious practice.

Religious freedom is therefore not a private preserve, an isolated set of observances, odd, quaint, and of faint importance to our nation. No, upon this fundamental freedom rests the whole of our republic. Among the Founders, John Adams was clearest that our design for government would not and could not succeed without religion. "Our system of government," he said, "was made for a moral and a religious people and is wholly inadequate to the government of any other." Our system depends on citizens seeing and carrying out first their duties to God, then to their family, country, and neighbors.

A free people cannot have a government empowered to do

what they must do themselves. Our nation stands at a point in history where we must see a spiritual, moral, and cultural renewal in our nation. Over the past fifty years, much progress has been made in building new bonds of solidarity in the church and in society, but looking around us today, can we truly say that our nation has transcended the racial divide? Only the church can deliver our nation from the fires and fetters of racial hatred. On this question, we come not to demand more of government but more of ourselves.

We cannot turn the corner on rebuilding families, marriages, neighborhoods, health-care systems, small businesses, or any other element of our society if we do not march together—"neither Jew nor Greek, there is neither slave nor free, there is no male or female," but "are all one in Christ Jesus" (Galatians 3:28 ESV). As these words of the apostle Paul remind us, religious freedom is ultimately not a matter of exemptions and accommodations, acts of civil disobedience or gestures of resistance. Our freedom is *for* something. And our religious freedom is for everything: for overcoming ancient enmities, for peace in our hearts and in our homes, for reconciliation and growth in our communities, for individual and neighborhood development, for respect and cooperation among neighbors, and for the truth that really does set us free.

Let us join together in a renewed pledge to ensure that our nation remains one nation under God, where faith, family, and freedom flourish.

THANKS

☆ *Give thanks to the Father:* Praise you, Father, that your hand was most evident in the "birth" of our nation. Thank you that we still enjoy many of these freedoms of divine origin even as we struggle to maintain them. Help us, Lord.

CONFESSION

☆ *Listen for the Holy Spirit's prompting for confession:* Forgive us, Lord, as we have too often received your blessings and our freedoms in vain. At times, we have turned to government to do those things that we are called to do ourselves and for others. Forgive us, as we have not based our priorities first and foremost on you and your Word, then our families, neighbors, and country. Restore to my life your heart of loving you and my "nearest ones" even as I have been loved by you (see 1 John 4:19; Matthew 22:37–40).

PETITION

☆ *Join Jesus in prayers of petition:* Lord Jesus, even as you declare that it's truth that sets free, might we fully embrace "thy word" as truth (see John 8:32; 17:17). Even as you birthed marriage with divine intent, might it be true that the fidelity and testimony of my marriage will be a witness of you and your love (see Ephesians 5:28–32). Even as you have declared that children are gifts from the Lord, might I train and nurture them to walk in your ways (see Psalm 127:3).

WORD

☆ *Proclaim promises from His Word:* "Righteousness exalts a nation ..." (Proverbs 14:34 NIV). Father, we humble ourselves to seek you and your righteousness; restore to us the narrow walk in your ways; return to our nation a commitment to seek you and your voice and to obey your Word in all the affairs of life.

ENGAGE

☆ **Engage with other Jesus-followers in a lifestyle of prayer:** Join countless others on their knees for the Call2Fall prayer initiative the Sunday immediately prior to July 4 each year (Call2fall.com). Support the Freedom, Faith, and Family initiatives of the Family Research Council (frc.org), and involve your church and community in celebrating National Marriage week (nationalmarriageweekusa.org).

Love People P-5:
Spirit-empowered disciples minister His life and love to their nearest ones at home and with family.

DAY 18

Pray for Revival Among God's People

God has you where you are, at the right time, to accomplish the purpose of God.

What are we asking as we pray for our country? Ultimately, we are asking for the people of God to begin to experience the presence of Christ in a fresh way. All other results flow from that. Changed lives in the church as well as transformation in a culture come not from human effort but from the power of God made manifest in the lives of His people.

This isn't about praying for a better life or that things would go smoothly for us. Rather, it is about God and His purposes being accomplished. The acknowledged leader of the First Great Awakening, Jonathan Edwards, was fired by his congregation in the midst of revival. On a much larger scale, as the Third Great Awakening was taking place in the United States, the nation was dividing into the North and South, and war then tore the nation into pieces.

Some look to another Great Awakening in this nation as the solution to all our problems. That would be wonderful but unlikely. It is more likely to take place during great difficulties and even persecution. If awakening is widespread and lasting, it may well slow or delay the judgment of God against our sinful nation.

More importantly, another Great Awakening can empower the church to finish the task of world evangelization. All past revivals have had tremendous evangelistic outreach, and the one to come will as well. In addition, the repentance and humility that will be occurring in the body of Christ will be a key element in preparing the bride for the Bridegroom. Revival in the church can bring a restoration of New Testament purity, passion, and holiness.

What do we pray for on behalf of our nation? Certainly, the psalmist gives us a clear picture, and we would do well to use this in our prayers:

> Restore us again, God our Savior,
> and put away your displeasure toward us.
> Will you be angry with us forever?
> Will you prolong your anger through all generations?
> Will you not revive us again,
> that your people may rejoice in you?
> Show us your unfailing love, LORD,
> and grant us your salvation. (Psalm 85:4–7 NIV)

THANKS

☆ *Give thanks to the Father:* Thank you, Father, that in this very troubled world, my life is hidden with Christ and I have the privilege to follow you and be used by you as your Spirit changes me into your likeness.

CONFESSION

☆ *Listen for the Holy Spirit's prompting for confession:* Sadly, Lord, I can go through the motions of relating to you without truly seeking you with my whole heart; forgive me, restore me, and change me.

PETITION

☆ *Join Jesus in prayers of petition:* Lord, awaken me to your voice and revive my passion for you and your ways, that I might rejoice only in you. Deepen my love of you and your Word that I might walk humbly with you, sharing your likeness and love with others.

WORD

☆ ***Proclaim promises from His Word:*** Lord Jesus, might it be true of me that "the life I now live ... I live by faith in the Son of God, who loved me and gave himself for me" (Galatians 2:20 NIV). Holy Spirit, make this promise real in me, that I might be a living witness of the gospel's transforming power.

ENGAGE

☆ **Engage with other Jesus-followers in a lifestyle of prayer:** Join in the America Prays movement as thousands of churches partner together in 24/7 prayer for their community. Visit americaprays.org to sign up today.

Live the Word W-1:
Spirit-empowered disciples live the Word through frequently being led by the Spirit into deeper love for the one who wrote the Word.

DAY 19

Wake Up!

I know your works. Because you have limited strength, have kept My word, and have not denied My name, look, I have placed before you an open door that no one is able to close.

REVELATION 3:8 HCSB

While our nation's present condition is undeniable, much of the church sleeps. Spiritual lukewarmness is plaguing the church. Complacency and conflict categorize the church more than contrition and compassion. We place more emphasis on announcements and promotions than we do on prayer.

Now is the time for our churches to wake up. We need to

wake up from our slumber, indifference, and laziness. We need pastors to wake up to the fire of God and the anointing of God upon them while they preach God's Word weekly. We need our members to wake up and stand with their pastor, continually holding his arms up in prayer.

What holds back a fresh move of God's Spirit? The grim reality is that unforgiveness is one such major sin in the church. It builds a wall so thick one cannot break through it, so deep one cannot tunnel under it, and so high that no one can climb over it. While unforgiveness is choking the life of God's Spirit out of many of our churches, we need to believe again that the power of the gospel is greater than the wall of unforgiveness. While the wall of unforgiveness appears to be impenetrable, Jesus came to tear down every wall, including the wall of unforgiveness.

Pastor, forgive your members.

Members, forgive your pastor.

Pastor, forgive other pastors.

Church members, forgive other church members.

Freedom awaits you on the other side. We need to wake up to the oceans of God's grace. Open your arms to one another and to a world that needs the Lord Jesus Christ. Extend the hope of the gospel.

THANKS

☆ **Give thanks to the Father:** Father God, your example of extravagant grace and forgiveness is to be praised. My heart is moved with deep gratitude for how you have separated my sins as far as the east is from the west and remember them no more.

CONFESSION

☆ **Listen for the Holy Spirit's prompting for confession:** "Come to me, all you who are weary and burdened, and I will give you rest" (Matthew 11:28 NIV). Maybe you are weary of unforgiveness; perhaps you are weary of seeking fulfillment in what you have acquired, achieved, or accomplished; maybe you are weary of succumbing to the world's demands; or perhaps you are weary of trying to live in your own strength, wisdom, or power. Holy Spirit, cleanse and forgive me; change and empower me.

PETITION

☆ *Join Jesus in prayers of petition:* As I meditate on the wonder of your forgiveness and your promise of rest, my heart is moved to ask for you to prompt and empower me to forgive others. Specifically, I choose now to forgive _____. I want to return to intimacy with you because I know that's where I will find strength and renewal for my soul.

WORD

☆ *Proclaim promises from His Word:* "Take my yoke upon you and learn of me" (Matthew 11:29 NIV). This is your invitation to join Christ to impart His life and love to others. Listen as He speaks to you.

   ° Who among your family and friends might He be forgiving and accepting ... but He does so without you?
   ° Who in your workplace or community is He burdened about ... but you are not?

ENGAGE

☆ **Engage with other Jesus-followers in a lifestyle of prayer:** Form prayer triplets to pray together weekly and help each other be accountable to not only forgive offenders but to pray for them, make a list of names, and pray specifically for the salvation of souls. Visit projectpray.org for information on establishing other prayer strategies.

Live the Word W-6:
Spirit-empowered disciples live His Word through consistently encountering Jesus in the Word for deepened transformation in Christlikeness.

DAY 20

What Are You Remembering?

Our nation is facing a crisis of hope.

Then his people recalled the days of old,
    the days of Moses and his people—
where is he who brought them through the sea,
    with the shepherd of his flock?
Where is he who set his Holy Spirit among them … ?

—Isaiah 63:11

*R*ecalled is a powerful word. Especially in this situation, the recollection of what God had done in the past led to a revival among the Lord's people. It is so easy to forget the amazing works of God. That is never truer than when we get caught up in our own desires and ways. Forging ahead in our self-centeredness and sin, we forget all God has done in the past. So it was with the nation of Judah in Isaiah's day.

Now, however, God stepped in to punish their sin. Disaster ruled the day. The presence of God seemed far away. Sin did not seem so fun. Bit by bit, they began to remember that things used to be different. There was a time when God had led them through the godly leadership of Moses. There was a time when the Holy Spirit was present and made a real difference in their lives as individuals and as a nation.

Remembering past moves of God can be powerful. It can stir us to repentance and longing for a renewed sense of the presence of God. What are you remembering today?

THANKS

☆ ***Give thanks to the Father:*** Father, thank you for the gift of memory and for stories that have been passed down through the generations about the ways you have moved among your people. Thank you for stories of revival from past Great Awakenings in the United States and beyond. We praise you, Lord, that these stories can stir within our hearts a desire for similar awakenings. Thank you for challenging us to remind each other of your work in days past and of our great need today. May we recall those things that you would have us meditate on and pray over.

CONFESSION

☆ ***Listen for the Holy Spirit's prompting for confession:*** Speak Lord, I'm listening. Speak to me of my own self-centeredness. Remind me of days when I walked closer to you. Convict me of prayerlessness and a neglect of your Word. Change me, that I might become a "living letter" of your life and love.

PETITION

☆ ***Join Jesus in prayers of petition:*** Lord Jesus, just as you "became flesh and moved into the neighborhood" (John 1:14 MSG), so I long for your Word to be the explanation of my life. Move me from simply "knowing about" your truth to actually "doing" your Word.

WORD

☆ ***Proclaim promises from His Word:*** "You yourselves are our letter … read and known by everyone" (2 Corinthians 3:2 NIV). Holy Spirit, I yield to your work to change me through living God's Word. Remind me daily with the probing question, "What Bible verses did I experience today?"

ENGAGE

☆ **Engage with other Jesus-followers** in living a Spirit-empowered faith through personal devotions and small-group experiences that focus on loving the Lord, living His Word, loving people, and living His mission.

Visit greatcommandment.net/spirit-empowered-faith
for background on an age-stage model and resources
for a Spirit-empowered faith.

Live the Word W-2:

Spirit-empowered disciples live His Word through being
a "living epistle" in reverence and awe as His Word
becomes real in life, vocation, and calling.

DAY 21

Do You Need a Breakthrough Moment?

Our nation is facing a crisis of faith.

> Surely you are still our Father!
> Even if Abraham and Jacob would disown us,
> Lord, you would still be our Father.
> You are our Redeemer from ages past.
>
> —Isaiah 63:16

This passage has a powerful and much-needed statement of faith. Despite the poor spiritual condition of the nation and their estrangement from God, His people still spoke out by faith the truth that God was their Father. It was an essential step for them. There was every indication that the presence of God had been removed. God, earlier in this passage, declared that He was fighting against them. But in their repentance and sorrow, they held on to the truth of their covenant relationship with God as their Father. It was a breakthrough moment.

How often we need those breakthrough moments. Christians everywhere are living below their spiritual potential. Prayers go unanswered. God seems far away. We wonder about our relationship with Him. It is time to speak by faith who He is and who we are in Christ. When we wonder and doubt whether revival can ever come again, it is time to hold on to the truth of God's Word—that Jesus is coming for a bride who is pure and holy, adorned in white, a church that has been revived.

THANKS

☆ *Give thanks to the Father:* Father, how we love to call you by this name. You are indeed our eternal Father. We have been brought into your family through Jesus Christ, adopted as sons and daughters, and sealed with your precious Spirit. I praise and thank you for the wonder of my adoption into your family. You are my Father!

CONFESSION

☆ *Listen for the Holy Spirit's prompting for confession:* Change me, Holy Spirit, that I might quickly yield to you as I live out your Word. Forgive me when I doubt your Word and its hope that precedes believing faith (see Hebrews 11:1). Empower my testimony to proclaim the eternal truth of your Word as it transforms me from glory to glory.

PETITION

☆ *Join Jesus in prayers of petition:* Give us boldness to speak your Word by faith, even when the circumstances around us seem to go against it. We believe you, Lord, more than our circumstances. Thank you for the unchanging nature of your Word as you make my life a "living letter" that is known and read by others.

WORD

☆ *Proclaim promises from His Word:* "I have hidden your word in my heart, that I might not sin against you" (Psalm 119:11). I want my life to give witness of living out the truth of your Word. May the words of my mouth and the medications of my heart be pleasing to you. And help me to give witness to the power of your Word.

ENGAGE

☆ **Engage with other Jesus-followers** in truly experiencing the gospel of John. Visit relationshippress.om for a gifted chapter of the Experiential Gospel of John resource for living His Word.

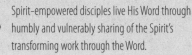

Live the Word W-4:
Spirit-empowered disciples live His Word through humbly and vulnerably sharing of the Spirit's transforming work through the Word.

DAY 22

Revival Fire

Let justice run down like water,
And righteousness like a mighty stream.
AMOS 5:24 NKJV

As we see our nation gripped by fear, our institutions crumbling, and communities erupting in flames and violence, our hearts are grieved and our spirits ache for God to pour out revival in our midst. We long for a great move of His Spirit that brings a reestablishment, restoration, and renewal of the family. We pray that hearts would be turned to Jesus, resulting in Christlike obedience and behavior. Yet, without repentance on the part of God's people passionately and humbly crying out for forgiveness and reverencing the name above all names, God is not compelled to respond with healing in our increasingly broken land.

Why is the church so impotent in this crucial hour? Why are we complacent and inactive? Why are we turning our heads away from the ugly realities of our culture, wringing our hands in despair and worry? Why are we hiding our lights under bushels rather than living out the life of Christ in us, the hope of glory?

The more widespread any revival movement becomes, the more transforming are the moral effects in the areas where God's holy fire has burned. How we long to see our nation burn with the fire of God instead of the fire of hatred and unrest and pain.

As we pray, God will reveal sinfulness that requires heartfelt repentance. Yet God's people do not know how to pray and generally balk at anything that looks like corporate prayer. Personal revival can certainly come; however, for lasting, sustainable moves of God to take place in the midst of God's people, we must come together—as families, as the local church, and in communities—crying out for God to restore us to right relationship with Him. Second Chronicles 7:14 promises that God will hear and answer and heal our land. How can we not take Him up on this amazing guarantee of His presence in our midst?

As God's people cry out to Him day and night, repenting of our sins and seeking His face for righteousness to be restored in our lives, our families, our churches, and our nation, God will hear and bring the healing we so desperately need.

THANKS

☆ ***Give thanks to the Father:*** Gracious Father, thank you that you have not left us without hope, but rather through the promise of your Word, we can be healed. I bless and praise you, that you continue to extend your loving-kindness to me as your Word is at work in my life.

CONFESSION

☆ ***Listen for the Holy Spirit's prompting for confession:*** Sadly, Lord, I too often resist deep conviction of sin, spiritual brokenness, and a holy fear of God. May your Spirit produce in me a "godly sorrow" that leads to brokenness and repentance (see 2 Corinthians 7:10). Holy Spirit, change and transform me into the likeness of Jesus.

PETITION

☆ ***Join Jesus in prayers of petition:*** Lord Jesus, we pray for deep cleansing, genuine repentance, and spiritual power to engulf pastors and Christian leaders. We ask for renewed pastors to lead united, prevailing prayer and a move of God in our day (see Ephesians 6:14–20).

WORD

☆ ***Proclaim promises from His Word:*** Believe God to be "at work" in His people to accomplish His will through spiritual hunger and fervent intercession. By His Spirit, He grants people—beginning with me—the genuine faith and the fervent desire for prayer: "For God is working in you, giving you the desire and the power to do what pleases him" (Philippians 2:13).

ENGAGE

☆ **Engage with other Jesus-followers in a lifestyle of prayer:** Pray and help lead your church to become a House of Prayer, crying out for revival, awakening, and national renewal. Visit The Family Research Council website frc.org or watchmenpastors.org for resources and ways to encourage preaching on moral issues from a biblical perspective, focusing on Christian citizenship a least one Sunday a year, and how to partner with three or more people for prayer and united action, leading efforts to make a positive impact in your community, state, and our nation.

Live the Word W-6:

Spirit-empowered disciples live His Word through encountering Jesus in the Word for deepened transformation in Christlikeness.

DAY 23

A Lifestyle of Forgiveness

"I have decided to stick with love.
Hate is too great a burden to bear."

MARTIN LUTHER KING JR.

I s there someone you need to pray for today who has damaged or hurt you in some way? Perhaps you are angry with people you don't even know—politicians, workers on strike, someone who continually parks in your space, etc. Can you ask God to give you the grace to pray for them?

So often, an inability to pray for certain people blocks the fullness of God's blessing from entering our lives. We allow the "enemy" to give us feelings of hatred and a desire for revenge when Jesus says that we are to "love [our] enemies" and "pray for those who persecute [us]" (Matthew 5:44). This is not an easy or simple assignment for many, but it is the way of the kingdom. If we desire a life that follows Christ, we must obey this directive from the one who prayed from the cross: "Father, forgive them; for they don't know what they are doing" (Luke 23:34).

Prayer compels us to connect with the Father through the Son, no matter who or what circumstances try to trip us up during our journey toward Christlikeness. Neglecting to love our enemies and pray for those who persecute us is sin. Psalm 66:18 reminds us, "If I regard wickedness in my heart, the Lord will not hear" (NKJV). Instead, Jesus tells us, "If you forgive those who sin against you, your heavenly Father will forgive you" (Matthew 6:14).

May the ministry of forgiveness continually be part of our lives as we step into each day's journey so that God will be honored and glorified among His people.

THANKS

☆ ***Give thanks to the Father:*** I bless and praise you, holy Father, that while I was yet a sinner, you allowed your

Son to die in my place that I might receive the miracle of forgiveness and eternal life; may I never get over the wonder of this love.

CONFESSION

☆ *Listen for the Holy Spirit's prompting for confession:* Speak, Lord, as I listen quietly for those individuals or groups of people I choose now to forgive; convict me with a sorrow that produces change in me and freedom for those I have harbored resentment against.

PETITION

☆ *Join Jesus in prayers of petition:* Even, Lord Jesus, as you have declared "Father, forgive them," I join you in declaring the same. By the power of your Spirit, I choose to live life, forgiving others as I have been forgiven.

WORD

☆ *Proclaim promises from His Word:* "Get rid of all bitterness, rage, anger, harsh words, and slander, as well as all types of evil behavior. Instead, be kind to each other, tenderhearted, forgiving one another, just as God through Christ has forgiven you" (Ephesians 4:31–32). Holy Spirit, empower my life with kindness, tenderheartedness, and compassion toward all as a sign of forgiveness, giving witness to the power of the gospel.

ENGAGE

☆ **Engage with other Jesus-followers in living a lifestyle of prayer:** Discover ways that local movements of united prayer can seek to pray for every person throughout entire communities in order to prepare the way for great gospel harvest and community transformation. Visit waymakers.org for resources and prayer guides that will help you and your prayer partners envision and believe God for ways united prayer can prepare communities for evangelization and spiritual

awakening through a practical passion for the greater
glory of Christ and fruitful lives in God's kingdom.

Live the Word W-7:
Spirit-empowered disciples live the Word through a life
explained as one who experiences Scripture.

DAY 24

Secrets Made Known by the Light

*"Silence in the face of evil is itself evil: God will not hold us
guiltless. Not to speak is to speak. Not to act is to act."*

DIETRICH BONHOEFFER

Jesus said, "For nothing is hidden that will not become evident, nor anything secret that will not be known and come
to light" (Luke 8:17 NASB). The answer to our prayers is beginning to germinate. Revival, which once seemed somewhat
dormant, is beginning to show signs of life. Revival is on its
way! How do we know that?

As churches begin to raise the bar on prayer, there is one
thing we often see: "hidden things coming to light." Typically,
as a church begins praying more and asking for the transforming work of Christ in its midst, suddenly the truth comes to
light that an elder has been sexually abusing his daughter (or
some other sad and grievous sin). Or perhaps the marriage of
a key couple in the church suddenly implodes, even though
there were no visible signs of trouble. Why would we see this?

First, satan wants to see if a church has the fortitude to
withstand the results of prayer. He tries to make prayer so

messy that people back away from serious intercession. Fear and pain brought on by unpleasant exposures can cause people to cease praying for transformation. Second, if Jesus Christ is going to release His transforming power in a church, all masks must come off. He will allow those hidden things to come to light so that repentance, forgiveness, and healing can take place.

Many have been praying for revival for decades. Others are just now recognizing that it is getting darker and darker in our nation and that a fresh move of God is the only answer. Prayer—a unified crying out in desperation—is the key. Consequently, more and more people are engaging in prayer.

God is beginning to move in response to our cries. But first He will move in a way that purifies His bride, the church. He is allowing the falseness, pride, dabbling in the world, and secret sins in the church to be exposed. Why? So repentance will follow and healing can come. Then He can pour out His Spirit in a powerful way to cause His church to once again be a light in a dark place.

THANKS

☆ **Give thanks to the Father:** Thank you, Father, that as we continue to pray for revival in the church and spiritual awakening in our nation, you can be counted upon to shake manmade idols and bring to light secret things. I praise you for your righteous love that purifies my heart and sharpens my kingdom testimony in this world.

CONFESSION

☆ **Listen for the Holy Spirit's prompting for confession:** Holy Spirit, use the building turmoil in this nation for God's glory—to purify and revive the church and to bring many people to a personal relationship with you. I turn from my lukewarm attitude and compromising spirit. Please purify my life and engage me more and more in the harvest.

PETITION

☆ *Join Jesus in prayers of petition:* Jesus, my heart joins yours in longing for a spirit of repentance and humility to move on your people, so we can, in turn, be the salt and light you call us to be. Begin with me.

WORD

☆ *Proclaim promises from His Word:* "Walk in the light while you can, so the darkness will not overtake you. Those who walk in the darkness cannot see where they are going" (John 12:35). Holy Spirit, I yield my life to a daily walk in the light of God's Son, God's Word, and God's people through:

- ○ Fresh encounters with Jesus (see John 8:12).
- ○ Frequent experiences of Scripture (see Psalm 119:105).
- ○ Faithful engagement in fellowship with Christ-followers (see Matthew 5:14).

ENGAGE

☆ **Engage with other Jesus-followers in a lifestyle of prayer:** You are not alone in pursuing transformation in your life, church, and community. Visit missionamerica.org to learn more about ministry networks who are connecting together to help facilitate communication, relationships, and cooperation as an important key to multiplying the power of the Spirit—particularly among those who share a common purpose or serve a specific demographic group or community.

Live the Word W-3:

Spirit-empowered disciples live His Word through yielding to the Scripture's protective cautions and transforming power to bring life change.

DAY 25

Look Around and
See the Lostness

Our nation is facing a crisis of eternal priorities.

The polarization and division in our nation and the multiple crises and the extreme division occurring in the churches of our nation are a strong call from God to us: "Come back to me!" We need to wake up! We must come back to God! Now is the time for us to repent, return to the Lord, plead for mercy, and call our nation back to God.

The church cannot call our nation to repent until the church repents. We need to repent of our prayerlessness. We need to repent of our unbelief. We need to pray for ourselves to get right with God and right with one another. The stakes couldn't be higher.

The stakes couldn't be higher in our nation. Now is the time for the church to be the church, praying for our nation. Our hope cannot be in politics, parties, positions, possessions, or people. Our eyes need to be fixed on Jesus alone. Our hope is not in Washington, DC or your state capital, but in the cross and resurrection of Jesus Christ. God can do anything, anytime, anywhere, with anyone. God can do more in a moment than you could ever do in a lifetime.

Our nation is lost without Jesus Christ. We are a nation of people who are lacking meaning and purpose. Religion is not the way to God. Morality is not the way to God. Goodness is not the way to God. Money is not the way to God. There are not multiple ways to God. There is only one way, and it is through Jesus Christ alone. Jesus Christ is the only way to know God personally.

How much longer will people keep killing other people? How much longer will people keep abusing others? How much longer will people keep filling their bodies with drugs and alcohol? How much longer will people keep devaluing others? How much longer will all of this continue?

People who are spiritually lost without Jesus Christ will continue to live like they are spiritually lost without Jesus Christ. That is why our nation needs Jesus more now than ever before.

THANKS

☆ ***Give thanks to the Father:*** I offer blessings and praise to you, Father God, for entrusting your people with the gospel. I am grateful you have entrusted me with the good news of Jesus.

CONFESSION

☆ ***Listen for the Holy Spirit's prompting for confession:*** Forgive me for not clearly being salt and light to those around me who need Jesus. Forgive me for not speaking of Jesus as our only hope. Change me and empower my witness for Jesus.

PETITION

☆ ***Join Jesus in prayers of petition:*** "Jesus told him, 'I am the way, the truth, and the life. No one can come to the Father except through me'" (John 14:6). Lord Jesus, evangelism cannot be separated from prayer. Lead me often to pray into this spiritual lostness. Remind me often that prayer cannot be separated from evangelism, and I am called to proclaim Jesus as the only way.

WORD

☆ ***Proclaim promises from His Word:*** "… we were well-pleased to impart to you not only the gospel of God but also our own lives, because you had become very dear to us" (1 Thessalonians 2:8 NASB). Holy Spirit, lead me to those needing Jesus and empower my witness of life and words.

ENGAGE

☆ **Engage with other Jesus-followers in a lifestyle of witness:** Visit lifeway.com, cru.org (formerly Campus Crusade for Christ), and Josh.org to access tools for helping you become more passionate about prayer and connecting people to Jesus Christ.

Live His Mission M-1:
Spirit-empowered disciples live His mission, imparting the gospel and one's very life in daily activities and relationships, vocation, and community.

DAY 26

Book of Acts Praying
The Best Practice for Church Growth

When they had prayed, the place where they were assembled was shaken, and they were all filled with the Holy Spirit and began to speak God's message with boldness.

ACTS 4:31 HCSB

Spiritual and numerical growth for churches has been under the magnifying glass for many years. There have been multiple strategies put forward to remedy the struggles and deficiencies associated with drawing people to Jesus and His church and then growing them into fully committed disciples of Jesus.

Consider the progression of the first numerical and spiritual growth of the early church in Jerusalem. What fueled the amazing addition of so many people in such a short time that they "filled the streets of Jerusalem with the teachings of Jesus"? All one needs to do is study the book of Acts to see the answer—kingdom-focused, corporate prayer.

In the beginning, 120 believers obediently met in an upper room to pray as Jesus had instructed them to do: "They all met together and were constantly united in prayer …" (Acts 1:14). This group of believers took Jesus at His word and waited prayerfully for the Holy Spirit that had been promised. The result, it was said, "turned the world upside-down for Jesus Christ." Here are some practices of the early church:

1. *Praying continually:* On the day of Pentecost, seven weeks after Jesus' resurrection, the 120 believers were still meeting together in one place. We must assume from Acts 1:14 that they were still in prayer. The promised Holy Spirit came. Jesus had told them: "And now I will send the Holy Spirit, just as my Father promised. But stay here in the city until the Holy Spirit comes and fills you with power from heaven" (Luke 24:49).

2. *Leaders who understand that prayer and the ministry of the word is the first priority:* During a time when they could have been lured into other activity, the leaders of the Jerusalem church said, "But we will devote ourselves to prayer and to the ministry of the word" (Acts 6:4 ESV). This is a simple and straightforward job description for church leadership, yet, over time, its simplicity has been perverted by worldly expectations and business models. Training in Bible colleges and seminaries has reduced prayer to a devotional silo expected of every believer and therefore not deemed worthy of academic study or as the foundational strategy for building a church or completing the Great Commission.

3. *Prayer in leadership decision-making:* During a season of prayer, Peter shared that the Scripture needed to be fulfilled and a new apostle was

chosen to take the place of Judas. After nominating two men, they all prayed for the right man to be chosen: "O Lord, you know every heart. Show us which of these men you have chosen" (Acts 1:24). Later, men at the church in Antioch had a similar experience: "While they were ministering to the Lord and fasting, the Holy Spirit said, 'Set apart for Me Barnabas and Saul for the work to which I have called them.' Then, when they had fasted and prayed and laid their hands on them, they sent them away" (Acts 13:2–3 NASB).

4. *Prayer-filled preaching of the Word:* When the prayed-up and prayed-for unlikely preacher Peter stood up and boldly proclaimed the truth of Jesus Christ, those who received that word were baptized. God added three thousand souls to the Jerusalem church on Pentecost.

5. *Prayerful lives devoted to the way of Jesus:* "They were continually devoting themselves to the apostles' teaching and to fellowship, to the breaking of bread and to prayer" (Acts 2:42 NASB). As this lifestyle of Jesus was lived out "with gladness and sincerity of heart" (Acts 2:46 NASB), "the Lord was adding to their number day by day those who were being saved" (Acts 2:47 NASB). Praying communities of believers see God do amazing things for God.

The bottom line is that praying leaders will multiply praying churches filled with praying disciples. Prayer is everyday life for the church of Jesus Christ.

THANKS

☆ *Give thanks to the Father:* Heavenly Father, with deep gratitude we celebrate the powerful simplicity of devoting ourselves to "prayer and ministry of the Word" as the hope of gospel expansion.

CONFESSION

☆ *Listen for the Holy Spirit's prompting for confession:* Speak, Holy Spirit, as you desire to challenge me to a deepened walk with you. I repent of a shallow prayer life and at times missing the gospel opportunities you present.

PETITION

☆ *Join Jesus in prayers of petition:* Jesus, even as you pray for the world to know that we are your disciples by how we love, we commit to join you in this mission (see John 13:35). May the evidence of your love through me touch many with the gospel message.

WORD

☆ *Proclaim promises from His Word:* "Salvation is found in no one else, for there is no other name under heaven given to mankind by which we must be saved" (Acts 4:12 NIV). Lord, I yield to your eternal purposes in furthering the cause of Jesus and the gospel; I want to make my life count for eternity.

ENGAGE

☆ **Engage other Jesus-followers in a lifestyle of prayer and mission:** To connect with a network of local prayer leaders who are on a journey to bring prayer to the heart of all they do, visit projectpray.org/the-praying-church-movement. You'll also have access to national initiatives, a Prayer Trainers Program, and Prayerborne–Intercessor's Alliance.

Live His Mission M-3:
Spirit-empowered disciples live His mission through championing Jesus as the only hope of eternal life and abundant living.

DAY 27

Praying for Others to Come to Jesus Christ

"God is not calling us tonight to a playground or a sports arena—He is calling us to a battleground."

DR. BILLY GRAHAM

Are *you* praying for others to come to Jesus Christ? Do you call out specific names to God each day? Our nation needs Jesus Christ more now than ever before. Our hearts should be broken over the lostness of our nation and the world. Mocking it helps no one. Ignoring it does not make it go away.

Every genuine Christian needs to pray for others to come to faith in Jesus Christ.

THREE SPECIFIC WAYS TO PRAY FOR OTHERS TO COME TO JESUS CHRIST

1. Pray for the scales to fall away from their blinded eyes.

We cannot deny the reality of what Paul stated in 2 Corinthians 4:4, "In their case, the god of this world has blinded the minds of the unbelievers, to keep them from seeing the light of the gospel of the glory of Christ, who is the image of God" (ESV). Only through God opening their eyes and minds to the gospel will the unsaved see and hear the good news of Jesus Christ. We need to pray for them and appeal to God for this to happen.

When people do not know Jesus Christ, they are blinded to

the truth of their great need for salvation. Intercessory prayer that is intentional and continuous can see God remove the scales of blindness over their eyes and help them to see themselves as God sees them: Lost and in need of a relationship with Jesus Christ.

If we believe God can do anything with anyone at any time, then we can offer up prayers for the lost perpetually.

2. *Pray for God to engineer their circumstances to convince them they need Jesus Christ.*

Our God is sovereign and desires for all persons to come to Jesus Christ. He can engineer circumstances to help convince them that their number-one need is spiritual, and the answer is found in Jesus Christ alone.

We can pray like this because God wants all people to turn from living their own way, doing their own thing, and come to Him. "The Lord does not delay His promise, as some understand delay, but is patient with you, not wanting any to perish but all to come to repentance" (2 Peter 3:9 HCSB).

Therefore, we pray that our great sovereign God will engineer circumstances in their life that will show them their deep and desperate need for Jesus Christ.

3. *Pray for God to send someone to tell them about Jesus Christ.*

As you pray for them to hear about Jesus Christ, be willing to tell them yourself. In fact, ask God for the open door to share the good news of Jesus Christ with them and others. You might be the "someone" others are praying for to tell their friends or family members about Christ. Be faithful to ask God to use you to share Jesus with others.

May we be faithful to pray for all people to see our need for Jesus Christ and come to a personal relationship with Him.

THANKS

☆ **Give thanks to the Father:** Holy Father, I celebrate the kindness of your heart that "none should perish" and praise you for the gracious provision of your Son to make the good news available.

CONFESSION

☆ *Listen for the Holy Spirit's prompting for confession:* Forgive me as I have not prayed with passion for those outside of Christ; cleanse me from the busyness of human activity that hinders me from engaging more fully in gospel witness. Holy Spirit, I yield myself to live and share the eternal hope found only in Christ.

PETITION

☆ *Join Jesus in prayers of petition:* Lord Jesus, even as your heart is burdened for a harvest that is great but laborers are few, touch my heart; bring brokenness for the lost upon my heart. Holy Spirit, prompt and empower your prayer through me for those outside Christ. Speak now as I listen for who you would want me to engage in passionate prayer and courageous witness; I sense a specific urgency to pray for the scales of blindness to be remove from _____, _____, and _____.

WORD

☆ *Proclaim promises from His Word:* "'I looked for someone among them who would build up the wall and stand before me in the gap ...'" (Ezekiel 22:30 NIV). Lord God, even as you search to and fro for watchmen to stand in behalf of others and their destiny, my heart is yielded, and my spirit declares, "Here am I; send me." Engage me and empower me as you wish in this battle for eternity.

ENGAGE

☆ **Engage other Jesus-followers in support of Global Outreach Day:** Encourage others to embrace a vision that each year, on the last Saturday of May, every Jesus-follower will engage in gospel witness. Visit GlobalOutreachDay.com to learn more.

Live His Mission M-8:

Spirit-empowered disciples live His mission through attentive listening to others' story, vulnerably sharing their story, and a sensitive witness of Jesus' story as life's ultimate hope.

DAY 28

How to See the Gospel Spread and Flourish

They were amazed and began to recognize them as having been with Jesus.

ACTS 4:13 NASB

We love the story of the angel coming to Peter while he was asleep, chained between two guards. He tells Peter to get up, the chains fall off, and they walk outside (see Acts 12). But we don't want to miss some of the important aspects of this story other than the "Yay God!" feel-good miracle.

As the story opens, King Herod is beginning to seriously persecute the church. He arrests and executes James—a huge blow to the church, which must have delivered a strong statement to believers. He then goes after Peter and has him arrested. The assumption of the church had to be that Peter was to be executed too.

What do they do? Get a lawyer and take Herod to court? Whine on Facebook about how bad it is getting for believers in Jerusalem and the government should be fairer? Storm the prison? Nope. Acts 12:5 tells us that "the church was earnestly praying to God for [Peter]" (NIV).

That verse hints at two things: First, that this was strong, desperate, corporate prayer—people weren't allowed to take the request sheet home and hopefully remember Peter. They came together, realizing they needed a supernatural solution. Second, the prayer meeting was likely focused only on Peter and the growing problem of persecution. It was a vertically focused prayer time, not horizontally focused; it was not focused on the needs of the people in attendance, as most of our Western church prayer times are. Rather, it was focused upward—on God and His purposes.

THE RESULTS

Consider this: those who were praying didn't even have much faith! Remember what happened when Peter showed up at the door? The servant girl excitedly ran back into the house (without letting Peter in) and told the crowd Peter was at the door. "You're crazy," was the response. "That can't possibly be!" God answered with a miracle even though it appears they were still expecting Peter to go to trial. They were not expecting God to do something that immediate and miraculous.

The second major result most people miss is that God not only rescued Peter, which was the immediate answer to their prayers, but He changed the situation by soon removing Herod. The king died shortly thereafter. And then Scripture tells us that "the word of God continued to spread and flourish" (Acts 12:24 NIV). God used the agreement of those frightened believers to release a powerful miracle, remove a major obstacle, and further His kingdom.

THANKS

☆ ***Give thanks to the Father:*** Holy Father, we thank and praise you as the one who brings forth your will despite human frailties, for nothing shall thwart your plans! I praise you that your kingdom will come on earth as it is in heaven.

CONFESSION

☆ *Listen for the Holy Spirit's prompting for confession:* Forgive me, Lord, as I too often focus on the "horizontal" strategies of this world rather than the certain solutions of the kingdom; enlist my heart to prevail in prayer that you would show yourself strong on our behalf.

PETITION

☆ *Join Jesus in prayers of petition:* Lord Jesus, strengthen my faith to believe that any obstacle can be removed, miracles can happen, and the gospel ministry of your church can "spread and flourish."

WORD

☆ *Proclaim promises from His Word:* "The church was earnestly praying …" (Acts 12:5 NIV). Lord God, would you by your Spirit make this verse real for your people today? Would you gather us in united, prevailing prayer that your plans and purposes might come forth in our day? Come, Lord Jesus, come!

ENGAGE

☆ **Engage with other Jesus-followers in supporting Cry Out America on September 11:** Join together each year as we cry out for mercy, seeking a fresh work of His Spirit among us. Visit CryOutAmerica.us to learn more.

Live is Mission M-6:

Spirit-empowered disciples live His mission through bearing witness of a confident peace and expectant hope in God's lordship.

DAY 21

Behold the Lamb

"To Him who sits on the throne, and to the Lamb, be blessing and honor and glory and dominion forever and ever."

REVELATION 5:13 NASB

The choices we make today will impact our lives tomorrow. The choices we make and how we relate to the Lamb of God determines our destiny in this life and the next. How do you behold the Lamb of God? For how you behold the Lamb will change how you view all of life.

When we view the Lamb as the one who sits upon the throne, then we will live our life from that place of authority and power. And because He is on the throne, reigning supreme over all things, He is our hope that all things are going to work out one day. We have the choice to believe or not believe, to follow a dream or succumb to a nightmare, to lift our heads or walk in sorrow, to stay in the desert or march toward the Promised Land. We have a choice to live by faith or walk by sight, to look back or push forward, to stay silent because of sin or shout for joy because of grace.

WHERE IS THE LAMB?

For two thousand years, humanity asked the same question and then the answer came in John 1:29: "Behold! The Lamb of God who takes away the sin of the world!" (NKJV). Jesus is the Lamb. Even today, humanity cries out, "Where is the Lamb?" From all strata of society, men and women, children and elders, cry out for the Lamb. Let us rise up and respond with the answer of John the Baptist, "Behold! The Lamb of God."

God is now looking for people who will not only declare the identity of the Lamb and the provision of the Lamb, but who will hold on to the certainty of the Lamb's agenda so that they desire to do what's right even in the midst of criticism, persecution, and possibly imprisonment or death.

THE LAMB IS ON THE THRONE

Let this generation shake off the shackles of complacency and mediocrity while declaring, "Behold the Lamb! Behold the Lamb who brings forth righteousness and justice. Behold the Lamb who activates sanctification and service. Behold the Lamb who reconciles the message with the march, holiness with humility, and truth with love."

The apostle John saw the Lamb seated on the throne. Not only did the Father provide the Lamb, but He also seated the Lamb on the throne, which means the Lamb rules and governs. As long as the Lamb is on the throne, there is hope. Christ is our rock. As long as our rock, the Lamb, is on the throne, there is hope for our nation, hope for our children, hope for our faith, and hope for humanity. As long as the Lamb is on the throne, faith, hope, and charity will live.

THE LAMB IS OUR HOPE

Revelation 5:5 tells us that it is the Lamb who is capable of opening what others cannot open. And Revelation 5:9 tells us that it is the Lamb who produces a new song. Therefore, let us press forward with the agenda of the Lamb. Let us speak to the barrio and Beverly Hills, to those on Wall Street and Main Street, to all in this generation tired of partisan politics, tired of archaic nomenclature, tired of discord and strife, but hungry for righteousness and justice. Let us stand up and declare, "Behold! The Lamb of God who takes away the sin of all mankind."

THANKS

☆ **Give thanks to the Father:** Lord, thank you for giving me the boldness to declare that you are the Lamb of

God who takes away the sins of the world. Praise you that your Spirit empowers me to live for you and tell others about who you really are.

CONFESSION

☆ ***Listen for the Holy Spirit's prompting for confession:*** "Let us strip off every weight that slows us down, especially the sin that so easily trips us up" (Hebrews 12:1). Ask the Holy Spirit to examine your life so that you can rest in the bounty of God and then actively engage on mission with Him. Lord, speak to me about the areas of my life that might be weighing me down. Do I need to strip off bitterness, anger, envy, fear, insecurity, or shame? Do I need to let go of any sins—selfishness, pride, hatred, lust, or greed? Speak to me, Lord.

PETITION

☆ ***Join Jesus in prayers of petition:*** "Take my yoke upon you. Let me teach you, because I am humble and gentle at heart, and you will find rest for your souls" (Matthew 11:29). Imagine that Christ stands before you as the one who is love and invites you to come and take the other side of the yoke. Imagine now the whispered words of Jesus as the Lord would say to you, "I know there are times when you don't know how to live out my agenda, but you can learn from me. I can teach you. I know that you may not always understand what it means to live for me, but I will guide you. I know that there will be times that are hard for you, but rest in the truth that I am bearing the load with you. Would you come and take the other side of this yoke? Together let's live this life well."

☆ ***Pause and respond to His initiation.*** Lord Jesus, I am committed to join you and to learn from you. I especially want to join you in _____ .

WORD

☆ ***Proclaim promises from His Word:*** "And the corner-stone is Christ himself" (Ephesians 2:20). Meditate on the Lamb of God, who sits on the throne with outstretched arms and nail-pierced hands. He rules the earth and governs the heavens, and yet He welcomes you into His presence and is excited to love you. Because He is both ruler of all and lover of all, we have hope. Make plans to talk to a friend or family member about the hope that you experience when you embrace the truth that Jesus is on His throne as the ruler of all. Talk also about the hope you feel because you know that Jesus is the God of love and the corner-stone of your faith: "When I rest in the truth that Jesus is on His throne and in charge of our world, it makes a difference in my life because _____." And "When I embrace the truth that Jesus is the God of love and the Father of compassion, it solidifies my faith because _____."

ENGAGE

☆ **Engage with other Jesus-followers in a lifestyle of prayer:** Ask the Holy Spirit to prompt you and give you boldness as you declare to others that Jesus is the Lamb of God and that He takes away the sins of the world. Visit the National Hispanic Christian Leadership Conference website for ways to engage in compassionate evangelism with other ministries such as Convoy of Hope and One Day to Feed the World (nhclc.org/directives/compassionate-evangelism).

Live His Mission W-2:

Spirit-empowered disciples live His mission through expressing and extending the kingdom of God as compassion, justice, and forgiveness are shared.

DAY 30

Concentric Circles of Concern

We loved you so much that we shared with you not only God's Good News but our lives, too.

1 THESSALONIANS 2:8

I n the early days of the church, the gospel of Jesus Christ spread through authentic and meaningful relationships. It wasn't through campaigns or creative marketing, advertising, or going door to door. The gospel moved in waves of concentric circles, just like the waves created from a rock that's thrown into a pond move out in all directions, rippling further out.

The gospel is most effective when it begins within our own heart and has its way in our marriage, family, friends, and community—in that order. If you read through the New Testament, you will see the centrality of relationship. It is nothing profound, but it is just as natural as anything can possibly be. If something is genuine in my life and your life, the natural thing to want to do is to share it with those we know.

Relationship: It's the most important word in the English language.

EXPERIENCING THE PATTERN

Think of this pattern: Seven concentric circles on a whiteboard. These circles are like a target with a bull's-eye in the center, concentric circles. The circles represent the different relationships of our lives: Circle 1: Self; Circle 2: Family; Circle 3: Relatives; Circle 4: Friends; Circle 5: Neighbors and Associates; Circle

6: Acquaintances; Circle 7: Person X. The gospel moves on these contiguous lines—on lines of relationship. We are always training people in evangelism to go to Person X out there somewhere, but there is no prior relationship established with him or her. Lifestyle evangelism in the New Testament did not begin with Person X. It worked through relationships that had already been established. Let's look at a few.

ANDREW AND SIMON PETER

At the beginning of His ministry, Jesus began to choose disciples to follow Him. Andrew was the first. Notice what Andrew did when he first met Jesus (see John 1:35–42). When Andrew met the Savior of the world, Jesus the Messiah, his first instinct was to introduce his brother Simon (later named Peter) to Jesus. Though we don't read very much about Andrew, his brother Peter became one of the great leaders of the early church, and he wrote two books of the New Testament. What a contribution Andrew made to the kingdom of God! He carried the gospel of Jesus Christ to one in his immediate family through a relationship.

PHILIP AND NATHANAEL

Philip met Jesus and responded to Jesus' invitation to follow Him. He then went to Nathanael and brought his friend to meet Jesus too. When Nathanael met Jesus, he acknowledged that Jesus must be the Son of God and the King of Israel. Many believe that Nathanael is the same person who is called Bartholomew in the other three gospels. These two friends became two of the twelve disciples Jesus chose to be His closest companions. Philip carried the good news about Jesus through a relationship to his friend, and both their lives were forever changed (see John 1:43–51).

THE WOMAN AT THE WELL AND HER NEIGHBORS

Jesus took His disciples with Him on a journey through Samaria—a place that most Jews avoided because of prejudice. Beside the well at a city named Sychar, Jesus introduced

CONCENTRIC CIRCLES OF CONCERN · 83

Himself to a woman as the Christ (Messiah) and as the "living water." She believed Him (see John 4:28–30, 39–42). When she realized that Jesus was the long-awaited Messiah, she hurried back to town to share the good news with her neighbors and relatives. After only two days with Jesus, many believed in Him. One woman touched a whole city for Christ.

THANKS

☆ *Give thanks to the Father:* Lord, thanks for giving me a renewed passion for those closest to me. I want you to empower me to make disciples in my closest relationships as well as in those I have yet to meet. Thanks for helping me to consistently be reaching out with the life of Christ that you have placed within me.

CONFESSION

☆ *Listen for the Holy Spirit's prompting for confession:* Pause now and take a moment and consider the manner in which Jesus responded to the woman at the well. Remember how He acknowledged the woman's sin but treated her with respect, a person with intrinsic value in His eyes. The Father's loving plan is that our encounters with Jesus might lovingly transform us into His image. So take a moment and assess your heart.

  ○ What is your attitude toward sin and sinful people?
  ○ How do you treat those you know to be "sinners?"
  ○ Do you treat them like Jesus treated the Samaritan woman?

☆ When I consider my own heart and attitude toward other people, Lord, I realize that I do not always accept others as Christ does. I need to show more _____ (e.g., respect, acceptance, support) to _____ (name a specific person or group of people).

☆ Finally, make plans to experience James 5:16, confessing your wrong attitudes and responses to another person and then praying together: "Confess your sins to each other and pray for each other so that you may be healed" (James 5:16). Then ask the Holy Spirit to show you how you might accept others just as Jesus does—with love, compassion, and a desire for restoration.

PETITION

☆ ***Join Jesus in prayers of petition:*** "That you will know what is the hope of His calling, what are the riches of the glory of His inheritance in the saints …" (Ephesians 1:18 NASB). God's support, care, security, encouragement, patience, kindness, and acceptance are already within you. It is God's desire that you would share these riches with others in your concentric circles. Jesus, thank you for not only giving me the gift of salvation but also for filling me with some of your glorious riches. I'm especially grateful for your _____.

WORD

☆ ***Proclaim promises from His Word:*** "The love of God has been poured out within our hearts through the Holy Spirit who was given to us" (Romans 5:5 NASB). Reflect on your own experience of coming to follow Jesus. Can you recall the family members or friends who were there to tell you about the love of Jesus or who shared the gospel with you? Perhaps there was a specific person or group of people who were living examples of Christ's redemption. Reflect on your gratitude for this amazing experience with the Lord. "I feel grateful when I remember how God brought _____ into my life to show me and tell me about Jesus. Without him or her, I don't know where I'd be today."

☆ Share your responses with a prayer partner. Celebrate with one another about God's provision for His people.

ENGAGE

☆ **Engage with other Jesus-followers in a lifestyle of prayer**: "Speak, Lord, for Your servant is listening" (1 Samuel 3:9 NASB). Consider what the people in your circles might really need. Could they need God's support shared through you? God's care shared through you? God's kindness shared through you? Or any of His glorious riches listed above? Take a moment to be still before the Lord. Listen to His Spirit as you reflect on the relationships in your circles. Ask Him to reveal the changes that are needed. Holy Spirit, show me the riches that you have given to me, that are needed in the lives of others. Who needs your kindness, your support, your care, or your encouragement demonstrated through me today? Speak, Lord, for I am listening.

☆ Connect with Jesus-followers in the African Christian community as well as other Christian prayer networks from all over the world as God's instruments for united prayer and the blessing and healing of the land by visiting the African Strategic Leadership Prayer Network's site (aslpn.org). Live prayer trainings, valuable resources, and opportunities to unite in weekly prayer calls are provided.

Live His Mission M-4:

Spirit-empowered disciples live His mission through yielding to the Holy Spirit's role to convict others as He chooses, resisting expressions of condemnation.

Spirit-Empowered Disciple

Our nation is facing a discipleship crisis.

Our mission, which we call the Great Commission, was established with Christ's words on the Mount of Ascension: "Therefore go and make disciples …" (Matthew 28:19, see also vs. 20 NIV). What we often call the Great Commandment serves as a guide for our beliefs—our attitudes and actions—and how we go about this Great Commission. Jesus spelled out the Great Commandment, and love was front and center: "'Love the Lord your God with all your heart and with all your soul and with all your mind.' This is the first and greatest commandment. And the second is like it: 'Love your neighbor as yourself'" (Matthew 22:37–39 NIV).

In the light of our mission to make disciples, we can sometimes neglect that love is the guiding force that should govern how we pursue our mission. Paul admonishes us that without love, evidence of Spirit-empowerment is hollow and nothing but a clanging cymbal, profiting us nothing. It's as vital to have love guiding our mission as it is to have the Holy Spirit empowering us to complete it. Our mission is clear. Love is our guide. But what will it look like to make disciples through the lens of love?

THE LIFESTYLE OF DISCIPLESHIP

Spirit-empowered discipleship first requires a lifestyle of fresh encounters with Jesus. We must never get too busy working for Him that we lose our relationship with Him. Paul said, "I count all things to be loss in view of the surpassing value of knowing Christ Jesus my Lord" (Philippians 3:8 NASB). What kind of encounters with Jesus will mark the Spirit-empowered disciple? Here are just a few.

Jesus longs for our praise—praise from those He has blessed, healed, comforted, and encouraged. Therefore, one way to relate to Jesus is to reflect on His divine gifts and then give Him praise. Another way to have a productive encounter with Jesus is to be attentive to His voice—listen to Him. Many times, we think that to love Jesus and relate to Him means that we get busy doing things for him. Jesus is longing for us to do just what Mary did—give Him our undivided, focused attention. Luke wrote, "Mary … sat at the Lord's feet and listened to his teaching" (Luke 10:39 ESV). If we get quiet, we'll hear Him speak. His instructions never mislead us.

Secondly, to be a Spirit-empowered disciple, we need frequent experiences of Scriptures. We can't give out what we haven't received. If we love God, we'll love His Word. It's good to know doctrine and even to memorize the Bible, but it's more important to practice the Scriptures daily. That should be our goal. Peter teaches us, "Since you have in obedience to the truth purified your souls for a sincere love of the brethren, fervently love one another from the heart" (1 Peter 1:22 NASB). Are we practicing that daily? We can practice it by rejoicing with a friend when they have received a great blessing or by comforting a person in their sorrow or by weeping "with those who weep" (Romans 12:15). This is *doing the book*! Anyone who applies the Bible this way is achieving a Spirit-empowered outcome: "Being a living epistle in reverence and awe as His Word becomes real in my life."

Finally, a Spirit-empowered lifestyle requires faithful engagement with God's people. We must see people as God sees them or we will never love them as He loves them. We must see people as both fallen and alone. They have spiritual needs as well as relational needs. In Genesis 2:18, God says that Adam was alone, and it was "not good." Several verses before Adam and Eve fell into sin (see Genesis 3:6), God declared it was not good that Adam was alone. Ministering acceptance and removing a person's aloneness does not mean that we condone sin. Rather, it means that we look deeper to see people's needs. A clear vision for discipleship means that virtually every church meeting or event must be designed to enhance relationships and equip people to love God with all their hearts, serve God gladly and effectively, and multiply themselves in the lives of others.

THANKS

☆ ***Give thanks to the Father:*** Thank you, Lord, that you hear my cry because I want my life to be marked by the power of your Spirit. I want others to notice in me a relationship with you, your Word, and your people that is different. I praise you for empowering my witness for you with the love you have shown to me.

CONFESSION

☆ ***Listen for the Holy Spirit's prompting for confession:*** "Be happy with those who are happy, and weep with those who weep" (Romans 12:15). Reflect for a moment on the people around you who have recently experienced a positive event in their lives, but you missed out on rejoicing with them. Is there someone who's recently had a baby, completed a project, found a job, or completed a class? Ask God by His Spirit to lead you in actually "experiencing" Romans 12:15.

☆ Here's what expressing happiness might sound like:

　　º "I am so glad that you _____."
　　º "I'm excited for you _____."

☆ Choose one person who could benefit from your celebration as you listen to the Holy Spirit and then plan to "experience Scripture" and do the book. Celebrate with this person in a note, text, e-mail, or in person.

PETITION

☆ ***Join Jesus in prayers of petition:*** "That I may know Him and the power of His resurrection and the fellowship of His sufferings ..." (Philippians 3:10 NASB). Imagine from Luke 17, Jesus standing on the dusty road, one former leper has bowed before Him to give thanks, and He says, "Where are the other nine?" (Luke 17:17 ESV). What does it do to your heart to imagine Christ's disappointment? How does it make you feel to know that the Savior gave these men life, health, restoration, and blessing, and yet only one returned with a grateful heart? Tell Jesus how your heart responds to this incident. Encounter Him; relate to Him because of your love for Him: I want to be like the one who returned and thanked you. So please hear my gratitude. Lord, I am grateful today for how you have given me _____.

WORD

☆ *Proclaim promises from His Word:* "Therefore, accept each other just as Christ has accepted you so that God will be given glory" (Romans 15:7). Reflect on a time when another person looked beyond your sinfulness or fallenness and accepted you anyway. Celebrate the faithful engagement of God's people: "I remember a time when someone saw my faults and loved me anyway. I am so grateful for this person because he or she _____, and now ask God to empower your accepting of others in this same way."

ENGAGE

☆ **Engage with other Jesus-followers in a lifestyle of prayer:** "Open my eyes, that I may behold wonderful things from Your law" (Psalm 119:18 NASB). Pause to pray for God's Spirit to prompt and empower your "experiencing" Bible verses; then think of a person who doesn't know Jesus but who has recently had a positive event occur in his or her life. Live out Romans 12:15 with this person. You'll be amazed at the connection that's built, the love they will experience, and the openness to the gospel that will result. Visit preach2engage.com for resources on experiencing Scripture.

Live His Mission M-9:
Spirit-empowered disciples live His mission through pouring their life into others, making disciples who in turn make disciples.

ABOUT THE
GREAT COMMANDMENT NETWORK

The Great Commandment Network is an international collaborative network of strategic kingdom leaders from the faith community, marketplace, education, and caregiving fields who prioritize the powerful simplicity of the words of Jesus to love God, love others, and see others become His followers (Matthew 22:37–40, Matthew 28:19–20).

THE GREAT COMMANDMENT NETWORK IS SERVED THROUGH THE FOLLOWING:

Relationship Press – This team collaborates, supports, and joins together with churches, denominational partners, and professional associates to develop, print, and produce resources that facilitate ongoing Great Commandment ministry.

The Center for Relational Leadership – Their mission is to teach, train, and mentor both ministry and corporate leaders in Great Commandment principles, seeking to equip leaders with relational skills so they might lead as Jesus led.

The Galatians 6:6 Retreat Ministry – This ministry offers a unique two-day retreat for ministers and their spouses for personal renewal and for reestablishing and affirming ministry and family priorities.

The Center for Relational Care (CRC) – The CRC provides therapy and support to relationships in crisis through an accelerated process of growth and healing, including Relational Care Intensives for couples, families, and singles.

For more information on how you, your church, ministry, denomination, or movement can be served by the Great Commandment Network write or call:

Great Commandment Network
2511 South Lakeline Blvd.
Cedar Park, Texas 78613
#800-881-8008
Or visit our website: www.GreatCommandment.net

Scan here to read about the contributing authors.

Scan here for more information about Spirit-Empowered Faith and Disciples.

Scan here for suggested resources.

BroadStreet Publishing® Group, LLC
Savage, Minnesota, USA
BroadStreetPublishing.com

31 DAYS OF PRAYER FOR MY NATION (Abridged)

Copyright © 2018 Great Commandment Network

978-1-4245-6186-5 (softcover)

Stock or custom editions of BroadStreet Publishing titles may be purchased in bulk for educational, business, ministry, fundraising, or sales promotional use. For information, please e-mail info@broadstreetpublishing.com.

Cover design by Chris Garborg at garborgdesign.com
Interior by Katherine Lloyd at theDESKonline.com

Printed in the United States of America

20 21 22 23 24   5 4 3 2 1